Fundraising and Nonprofit Marketing

This book provides a concise introduction to the latest research in the fundraising and nonprofit marketing field. It details the foundational studies in the area, reviews current controversies, outlines the main theories and models of fundraising, and presents suggestions for future research.

This second edition, as well as providing an update on recent significant contributions to the fundraising and nonprofit marketing domain, contains additional material on crowdfunding, the effects of disintermediation of charity giving, the consequences for fundraising of the Covid pandemic, public perceptions of the role of administrative expenditure by nonprofits, the influence of donors' levels of trust in charities, and disaster relief fundraising. The text guides the reader through the myriad of nonprofit marketing and fundraising research, summarises key findings and current thinking on fundraising strategies and processes, and offers conceptual insights into emerging themes. It highlights the studies that have the greatest contemporary importance and identifies gaps in knowledge that need to be addressed via further research.

Thus, the book provides an invaluable introduction to the literature on fundraising and nonprofit marketing and a convenient reference for students, for beginning researchers, and for more experienced academics and practitioners with interests in the nonprofit and fundraising field.

Roger Bennett is a Professor of Marketing at Kingston University, UK.

State of the Art in Business Research
Series Editor: Geoffrey Wood

Recent advances in theory, methods and applied knowledge (alongside structural changes in the global economic ecosystem) have presented researchers with challenges in seeking to stay abreast of their fields and navigate new scholarly terrains.

State of the Art in Business Research presents shortform books which provide an expert map to guide readers through new and rapidly evolving areas of research. Each title will provide an overview of the area, a guide to the key literature and theories and time-saving summaries of how theory interacts with practice.

As a collection, these books provide a library of theoretical and conceptual insights, and exposure to novel research tools and applied knowledge, that aid and facilitate in defining the state of the art, as a foundation stone for a new generation of research.

Ethical Consumption
A Research Overview
Alex Hiller and Helen Goworek

Strategic Human Resource Management, 2e
A Research Overview
John Storey and Patrick M. Wright

Sales Management
A Research Overview
Kenneth Le Meunier-FitzHugh and Kieran Sheahan

Fundraising and Nonprofit Marketing, 2e
A Research Overview
Roger Bennett

For more information about this series, please visit: www.routledge.com/ State-of-the-Art-in-Business-Research/book-series/START

Fundraising and Nonprofit Marketing

A Research Overview

Second Edition

Roger Bennett

Routledge
Taylor & Francis Group

LONDON AND NEW YORK

Second edition published 2024
by Routledge
4 Park Square, Milton Park, Abingdon, Oxon, OX14 4RN

and by Routledge
605 Third Avenue, New York, NY 10158

Routledge is an imprint of the Taylor & Francis Group, an informa business

First edition published by Routledge 2019

British Library Cataloguing-in-Publication Data
A catalogue record for this book is available from the British Library

ISBN: 978-1-032-42809-3 (hbk)
ISBN: 978-1-032-42810-9 (pbk)
ISBN: 978-1-003-36440-5 (ebk)

DOI: 10.4324/9781003364405

Typeset in Times New Roman
by codeMantra

Contents

Preface to the Second Edition

In most western nations, the nonprofit sector contributes a significant amount to gross domestic product and often constitutes a primary foundation of a country's civil society. Nonprofit organisations (e.g., charities registered with state authorities, community associations, fundraising arts and cultural bodies, public service co-operatives, educational institutions, voluntary welfare associations) face issues that are both multi-faceted and complex. The manners whereby nonprofits deal with these issues are important for the societies in which they operate, given that the activities of nonprofit organisations (i) impact heavily on social well-being, (ii) strengthen civil society, (iii) improve the lives of those in need and, collectively, (iv) have numerous implications for public policy.

A minority of nonprofit organisations are financed entirely by governments, by corporations, or by philanthropic foundations, and hence, do not need to solicit funds. Likewise, some nonprofits are fortunate enough to have been endowed with initial levels of resources sufficient in size to enable them to finance all their activities; both immediately and in the longer term. However, the overwhelming majority of nonprofits need to raise funds. It is entirely appropriate therefore for the current text to concentrate on the fundraising function. Donations are obtained from individuals, from businesses, from foundations or philanthropic institutions, and possibly from various government agencies. The effective procurement of donations from these sources utilising the latest fundraising methods, practices, and techniques is essential for all fundraising organisations, and for most nonprofits is an existential necessity. It follows that extensive, robust, and intellectually rigorous research into the nonprofit sector, and especially into nonprofit marketing and fundraising, is societally necessary and academically worthwhile.

Fundraising and Nonprofit Marketing: A Research Overview provides a concise introduction to the latest research in the fundraising and nonprofit marketing field. It details the foundational studies in the area, reviews current controversies, outlines the main theories and models of fundraising, and presents suggestions for future research. This second edition, as well as providing an update on recent significant contributions to the fundraising and nonprofit marketing domain, contains additional material on crowdfunding, the effects of disintermediation of charity giving, the consequences for fundraising of the Covid pandemic, public perceptions of the role of administrative expenditure by nonprofits, the influence of donors' levels of trust in charities, and disaster relief fundraising. Further comments on the methodologies employed in fundraising research are also included together with extra recommendations on topics for future investigation.

The text guides the reader through the myriad of nonprofit marketing and fundraising research, summarises key findings and current thinking on fundraising strategies and processes, and offers conceptual insights into emerging themes. It highlights the studies that have the greatest contemporary importance and identifies gaps in knowledge that need to be addressed via further research. Thus, the book provides an invaluable introduction to the literature on fundraising and nonprofit marketing and a convenient reference for students, for beginning researchers, and for more experienced academics and practitioners with interests in the nonprofit and fundraising field.

1 Introduction

Any nonprofit organisation that is not wholly financed by government grants, by philanthropic foundations, by a business, or by its founders must engage in fundraising. Academically, the fundraising function lies within the wider domain of nonprofit marketing, which is a subject that covers a diverse range of issues and tasks and includes activities not immediately and *directly* concerned with fundraising. Examples of wider nonprofit marketing topics not necessarily related to fundraising include image and reputation management, public relations, attraction of volunteers, and the measurement of levels of satisfaction of an organisation's beneficiaries. Normally, however, the acquisition of funds is the main and final objective of all forms of nonprofit marketing work. Hence, this book is predominantly about research that relates to fundraising and fundraising methods and excludes, for example, matters pertaining to volunteer recruitment, public sector marketing, political marketing, social marketing, nonprofit involvement in civil society, and nonprofit governance. The text acknowledges the seminal literature upon which later studies have been constructed, but, in the main, the book concentrates on key recent investigations, on the latest research into management orientations associated with fundraising, on current debates surrounding theories and models of fundraising, on fresh approaches and ideas, and on evolving research themes.

This first chapter introduces the reader to the overall landscape of fundraising and nonprofit marketing, beginning with an outline of criticisms of the practice (which have been vociferous) and a summary of the research literature that responded to attacks. Elemental criticisms of nonprofit marketing and fundraising have been that it wastes money, is unethical, employs dubious fundraising methods (notably 'chugging' [slang for 'charity mugging', i.e., the use of paid external agencies to obtain bank standing-order donations from passers-by in street locations]), and is under-regulated. Research relating to each of these matters is examined below, together with studies concerning the alleged 'commercialisation' of the nonprofit sector and the associated claim that today too many nonprofits undertake activities that should be completed by the state.

DOI: 10.4324/9781003364405-1

Chapter 2 examines key contributions to fundraising research which explored the questions of 'why do people donate' and 'what characteristics describe the "giving type"'? Many investigations have sought to answer these questions, and there exists a large body of research literature in the field. Models representing specific 'theories of giving' that have been offered by leading nonprofit researchers are outlined in Chapter 2 and are followed by a discussion of why individuals choose to donate to particular types of cause (e.g., giving to an animal sanctuary rather than to a prisoner rehabilitation charity). The chapter also explores the subject of giving by businesses, an area that has been researched voluminously in recent decades. Finally, Chapter 2 surveys seminal research papers on corporate philanthropy, on cause-related marketing, and on business sponsorship of nonprofit organisations.

The third chapter discusses theories and practices relating to donor retention, opening with an account of foundational research in the area of relationship marketing and progressing to an analysis of research into the problems of 'slacktivism' and the tendency of relationship marketing to attract large numbers of unprofitable donors. The chapter then examines research in the fields of nonprofit advertising and branding. Branding is a crucial nonprofit marketing activity with multiple implications for fundraising. Accordingly, Chapter 3 reports the outcomes to major research studies completed on, among other things, (i) attempts to define nonprofits' 'brand personalities' and (ii) the development by researchers of measures of nonprofits' levels of 'brand orientation'.

Chapter 4 deals with research into online giving and the use of social media for fundraising, with the solicitation of donations via mobile devices, and with the opportunities that new media provide for the introduction of innovative fundraising practices. The chapter also examines research undertaken into 'major gift' fundraising, legacy fundraising, and the use of sporting events to attract donations. Chapter 5 provides a general conclusion, reflections, and suggestions for future research in the fundraising and nonprofit marketing domain.

Does nonprofit marketing have a darker side?

The current chapter begins with a discussion of the question of whether nonprofits spend too much on marketing. In fact, research cannot provide meaningful answers to this query as it is not technically possible to measure accurately the average proportion of income allocated to marketing by any given sample of nonprofit organisations. This is due to differing applications of accounting standards and delays in reporting information and because marketing expenditures are, for accounting purposes, frequently merged with 'general administration'. (The term 'overhead' is often used to describe the conflation of advertising, general marketing and public relations, managerial salaries, and spending on administration.) Studies have established, nevertheless, that there exist large inaccuracies in public perceptions of the percentages of nonprofits' incomes that go to beneficiaries rather than to management and marketing. A valuable analysis of this matter was presented by Sargeant, Lee, and Jay (2009), who reported that the accounts of the top 500 charities in England and Wales indicated that, on the average, these 500 organisations devoted about 80% of their incomes directly to beneficiaries leaving the remaining 20% for spending on everything else, including marketing and administration. Other investigations have confirmed that about 80% of the average fundraising nonprofit is spent on services to beneficiaries. Yet, studies reveal that many people believe that around *half* of a typical charity's income is spent on administration (for details of relevant investigations, see Sargeant, Ford, and West [2000] and Bennett and Savani [2003]). An example of these studies was that of Sargeant et al. (2000), which questioned 980 charity donors and 249 non-donors about their estimates of how much of a person's gift to a charity would be spent on beneficiary-related programmes. On average, the non-donors believed that only 45.5% of the money donated to a charity would be spent on philanthropic activities and 54.5% on management and marketing. Even active givers assumed that just 67% of revenues went to the good cause.

This line of research was pursued in an exploration of the determinants of the accuracy of public perceptions of charity expenditure on administration undertaken by Bennett and Savani (2003) who, via a survey of 286 people, found that assessments were more realistic among individuals who (i) had a substantial level of knowledge about the charity sector in general and (ii) had received large amounts of information concerning the specific charities they supported. It seemed, therefore, that information provision stimulated cognitive effort which led to more accurate evaluations. People with substantial amounts of knowledge about charities gave more accurate assessments of charities' levels of spending on marketing (which for the charities in the sample in fact averaged 7%) and made better predictions of which attributes of a particular charity 'went together' (e.g., high rate of growth of income and high growth of spending on marketing). However, most of the participants in the study believed that extensive spending on marketing by charities was 'bad'. The authors concluded that the provision of information on charities was the key to improving the precision of people's estimates of how much of their incomes charities spent on marketing. Likewise, a survey of 1,801 participants completed by Qu and Daniel (2021) suggested that the provision of information which described the purpose of higher overheads in terms of building long-term organisational capacity caused many donors to choose to give, despite their knowledge of a charity's relatively high spending on overheads.

The question of what constitutes the 'right' level of administrative overheads that a charity should report to the public was addressed by Allred and Amos (2023) via two studies, each involving around 200 US donors. Allred and Amos (2023) concluded that the approximate maximum that donors would accept was 25%. Anything reported above 25% was liable to decrease

---

Box 1.1   Research opportunities: public perceptions of nonprofit spending on marketing

Research on this topic, by examining data objectively and by completing surveys of public opinion, has established that the perceptions held by many members of the public of the proportions of nonprofits' incomes spent on marketing and administration are wrong. Yet, there has been scant investigation of either the precise details or the antecedents of distorted perceptions. If, for instance, potential donors suspect that their contributions will be swallowed up by needless bureaucracy, then what exactly are the perceived components of a nonprofit's bureaucracy that cause offence? Conversely, some people might believe that it is perfectly reasonable for a nonprofit to spend a large part of its income on management and marketing. If so, who are these people and what are their characteristics? The fine details of the psychometric and socio-demographic profiles of this and of various other groups of potential donors who hold different assessments of the proportion of the average charity's income spent on beneficiaries need to be defined. Also, what are the influences on the views of each group of, for example, a nonprofit's image and reputation, type of cause, size, age, and other features. The *contexts* in which perceptions, attitudes, and opinions are formed are also worthy of investigation. What, for example, are the influences of family situation; of friends, relatives, and workmates; of housing and employment situations; and/or of geographical location? Does a person's assessment change over time, and if so, how and why? Do particular life experiences alter an individual's assessment of the proportion of a nonprofit's revenues spent on beneficiaries? An interesting issue is the inconsistency of some people's attitudes in that, on the one hand, they want nonprofits to be managed efficiently and effectively by trained and competent professional administrators, while, on the other hand, they demand that nonprofits spend hardly any of their revenues on professional administration. How do such attitudes arise and how can they be altered?

---

donations and hence required special promotional activity in order to reduce, in the authors' words, 'overhead aversion effects'. According to three studies undertaken by Newman, Shniderman, Cain, and Sevel (2019) (with sample sizes of 203, 297, and 320 adults, respectively), a donor's willingness to accept a charity's (perceived) relatively high expenditures on overheads depended in part on the person's level of commitment to the charity's cause because high commitment induced in the donor positive evaluations of the organisation's intentions.

A charity's response to donors' dislike of 'high' overheads can have negative organisational consequences, notably if the response gives rise to a 'nonprofit starvation cycle', i.e., the phenomenon that arises when a fundraising nonprofit organisation deliberately underinvests in its organisational infrastructure in order to present external images of low overhead expenditure. Schubert and Boenigk (2019) drew on financial data from 2006 to 2015 to investigate the extent to which the German nonprofit sector, as a whole, had experienced a starvation cycle, finding that reported overhead ratios had indeed fallen over the period. The authors noted how this could be particularly damaging with respect to cuts in spending on marketing, which is essential for raising funds. Lee (2021) examined US data for the year 2012, concluding that the proportion of marketing expense in US charities' total expenditures was positively and substantially associated with the proportion of donations within their total revenues. Reducing marketing activities could therefore be counterproductive.

Ethicality of fundraising practices

A second criticism levied against nonprofits is that some of their fundraising practices have been (and continue to be) unethical. In the UK, for example, fundraising charities have been accused of menacing the public with demands for money, of using psychologically disturbing images in advertisements, of coaxing donations from individuals who cannot afford them, of bombarding households with requests for gifts, and of other malpractices described in later sections of this book. An interesting example of an ethical critique of a charity campaign was provided in a study by Gies (2021), who reported complaints registered by a group of breast cancer survivors who objected to the 'Brave the Shave' appeal made by the UK charity 'Macmillan Cancer Support'. The appeal had encouraged members of the public not living with cancer to seek sponsorship to shave off all their hair and share the event on social media. The objecting group condemned the campaign as being insensitive, shallow, and offensive, on the grounds that there was nothing 'brave' about a healthy person shaving, whereas a cancer patient's experience of hair loss could be traumatic. *Real* bravery was said to relate to a person with cancer undergoing chemotherapy and/or radiotherapy and enduring all its possible debilitating side effects. The dissenting group also disliked the 'party atmosphere' (beers, barbecues, etc.) shown in advertisements accompanying the appeal. They also pointed out how compulsory shaving of the head has been well publicised as a publicly humiliating punishment (usually for women) in war situations. Nevertheless, Macmillan continued with the campaign arguing, according to Gies (2021), that it was financially successful and provided resources for the charity's services.

A major study into the ethicality of fundraising was undertaken by MacQuillin (2016), who concluded that it was genuinely possible for nonprofits to attain an 'ethical balance' with donors when raising funds. Donors did not want to be pressurised or pestered; yet, fundraisers had to solicit gifts on behalf of their organisations' beneficiaries. Fundraisers owed a duty of care to both donors and beneficiaries, so it was inevitable that tensions would arise between, on the one hand, donors' wants (e.g., not wanting to be contacted too frequently or to be pestered to give higher amounts), and on the other hand, beneficiaries' requirements that fundraisers acting on their behalf maximise a nonprofit's income. MacQuillin (2016) argued that fundraising was 'ethical' when it struck an appropriate balance between the two sets of demands and evidenced by outcomes where fundraising activities did not cause significant harm to either side.

MacQuillin extended his analysis of ethical issues in fundraising in a paper published in 2022 which reviewed extant literature in the field. The author examined 14 ethical theories, distinguishing between normative theories (which can be formulated in general terms and may be applied to specific situations), applied ethics (resolutions to particular ethical dilemmas in fundraising contexts), and professional ethics (i.e., aspirational principles as found in codes of practice). Few theories were characterised in the literature covered by the study as normative per se and applied ethical decisions often occurred in the absence of normative theory. MacQuillin (2022) described the paucity of normative ethics underpinning applied ethics in fundraising as an 'ethics gap'. Little empirical research has been completed in the fundraising ethics domain, and many opportunities for such research are available.

A further examination of the difficulty of balancing the interests of donors and beneficiaries was presented in a paper by Dean and Wood (2017), who noted how conflicts involving ethics could occur within nonprofit organisations between fundraisers (in Dean and Wood's [2017] interpretation, fundraisers represented donors) and managerial 'policy departments' (which were said to represent the need to raise as much money as possible in order to satisfy beneficiaries' requirements). Dean and Wood (2017) interviewed 23 fundraisers and managers about the 'battle between ethics and effectiveness' which the authors reported that some fundraisers had experienced when completing their work (p.1). Fundraisers were often called upon to devise campaigns that were deliberately intended to evoke feelings of guilt, fear, pity, and other negative emotions among potential donors. Campaigns of this type were necessary in order to raise large amounts of money in short periods of time. However, individual fundraisers were 'routinely internally conflicted about the rights and wrongs of using emotion in their work' (p.1). Hence, a strategic approach that balanced ethics with efficiency was needed when seeking to elicit negative emotions in donors. Fundraisers had to make careful balancing decisions. Yet, the authors observed that little was known about how individuals and fundraising teams actually made these decisions. Hence, it was imperative, Dean and Wood (2017) concluded, that further research be conducted into the ethical dimensions of fundraisers' decision-making processes.

Box 1.2   Research opportunities: fundraising ethics

In comparison with investigations of other topics, relatively little empirical research has been undertaken into fundraising ethics. Clearly, however, many research opportunities exist in the field. Research could attempt to discover the factors that cause nonprofits to undertake activities that could be regarded as unethical. Relevant antecedents might include managers' personal backgrounds and experiences, competitive intensity in the fundraising market, competitive instincts of individual fundraisers, the perceived severity of the consequences of an unethical act, or examples set by other nonprofits. A further research opportunity relates to fundraising managers' views of the usefulness of legislation intended to control fundraising behaviour, and how these views compare with those of the donating (and non-donating) public. It would be valuable moreover to examine whether there exists a single 'dominant logic' (i.e., a set of common norms, beliefs, and mental models) among nonprofit managers where ethical issues are concerned.

Case studies of how particular charities have dealt with specific ethical issues would be valuable. What considerations impel a charity to set up an in-house ethics committee and how do in-house ethics committees operate? To what degrees do charity boards of trustees discuss ethical matters that potentially affect an organisation? Are ethical concerns considered at all levels of a large charity or is 'ethics management' a compartmentalised activity, and if the latter, then why? Should government and regulatory bodies devise and impose mandatory ethical standards for charities over and above the general guidelines contained in the Fundraising Regulator's Code of Fundraising Practice? If so, what specific ethical issues should be covered?

Use of professional fundraising agencies

The third of the abovementioned criticisms of nonprofits' marketing activities, i.e., the use by large nonprofits of external professional fundraising agencies, has attracted much negative media and political attention, particularly vis-à-vis chugging. Research into the behaviour of paid external professional fundraisers is important in view of (i) the substantial financial value to nonprofits of the revenues obtained from face-to-face fundraising undertaken by external agencies and (ii) the level of opprobrium the practice has received, and hence, the reputational damage to the entire fundraising nonprofit sector that might result from bad publicity arising from the behaviour of paid external agencies.

Employees of professional fundraising businesses solicit potential donors in street locations or door to door, asking prospects to sign bank or credit card direct debits or standing orders for regular monthly gifts. In some years in the UK, around half a million donors have been recruited in this way, as have nearly one in five people who donate to charity via bank standing orders. However, lapse rates among recruits are extremely high. (Agencies refund a proportion of their fee if a donor cancels a standing order within a certain period, normally 12 months.) In many nonprofits, 50% of donors recruited face to face by external agencies lapse within the first year, and some nonprofits lose more than 80% of their face-to-face recruits within 24 months of acquisition.

Two studies by Bennett (2013a, 2013b) examined this issue among a sample of 669 agency-recruited donors to a UK healthcare charity. The first investigation estimated the time that a fresh agency-recruited donor would be required to remain with the charity (and how much extra a person would have to donate over and above a constant basic monthly donation) in order to recover the charity's recruitment and servicing costs. Recruitment and induction expenditures included the external agency's fee plus the nonprofit's donor registration and administration expenses, the costs of mailing welcome packs and brochures to the new supporter, plus ongoing communications costs. Results from the first study indicated that individuals who exhibited certain characteristics were significantly more likely to break even by the end of four years. The characteristics in question were whether a person had a strong sense of obligation to 'see through' an activity, was prone to enjoy relationships, felt involved with the charity's cause, was low in personal inertia, and tended to experience 'warm glow' (see Chapter 2) in consequence of giving. The second study explored the factors that potentially influenced the decisions of agency-recruited donors to cancel their standing orders shortly after signing a mandate. One hundred and ninety-six lapsed donors and 206 continuing donors to the healthcare charity were surveyed, the results revealing that three considerations significantly determined early lapse, i.e., a sample member's susceptibility to influence, the person's general tendency to overspend, and the perceived importance of the charity's cause.

Experimental studies of donors' perceptions of face-to-face paid fundraisers were undertaken by Waldner, Willems, Ehmann, and Gies (2020) and by Rau, Samek, and Zhurakhovska (2022). The first of these investigations involved respondents randomly assigned to either a face-to-face-fundraising group (65 participants) or a group of 60 people approached by letter. It emerged that face-to-face fundraising had a significant negative influence on perceptions of an organisation due mainly to perceived pressure, distrust, and obtrusion. In a study of 1.037 households, Rau, Samek, and Zhurakhovska (2022) found that fundraisers performed equally well regardless of whether they were paid or were charity volunteers. Donations were unchanged when donors were told that people making the ask were volunteers. Informing donors that fundraisers were paid did not decrease donations.

Box 1.3 Research opportunities: use of external fundraisers

A number of research opportunities arise in this area. It is relevant to note that successful chugging relies substantially on impulsive decisions made by target donors. Individuals differ in their tendency to act impulsively. The trait of impulsivity is multi-faceted and has been heavily researched in a number of disciplines. Possible connections between an individual's level of impulsivity and the person's susceptibility to an agency fundraiser's approaches are worthy of investigation. Another topic that merits future research relates to chuggers' desires to induce in people feelings of satisfaction at having done a good deed through signing a standing order. Thus, it would be useful to assess the importance to individuals of being able to experience a 'warm glow' in consequence of agreeing to make a monthly donation via a chugging experience. This could be examined in relation to the giving decisions of (i) impulsively inclined individuals and (ii) groups exhibiting other psychometric characteristics.

How much reflection and consideration do prospective donors devote to chuggers' requests during the few minutes of contact that occur between the two parties? Media reports suggest that many members of the general public dislike chugging, regarding the practice as intrusive, discourteous, and alarming. What are the sources of this animosity? If a member of the public who disapproves of chugging is confronted by a chugger who represents one particular fundraising nonprofit, might this deter the individual from giving to charity in general? Could chugging operations that are undertaken on behalf of a nonprofit in a specific sector (e.g., cancer care, animal welfare) damage the reputations of other nonprofits in the same sector that do not employ professional fundraisers?

Regulation of fundraising

Issue four of the previously mentioned list of criticisms of the nonprofit sector involves allegedly loose and inadequate systems for the regulation of fundraising organisations. Media accusations have been that, among other things, fundraisers pester the public with continuous requests for donations, that they routinely share supporters' contact information without permission, and that they generally lack accountability for their actions. The validity of some of these accusations was examined by Hind (2017), who concluded that (in the UK at least) many fundraising nonprofits had indeed engaged in inappropriate behaviour. However, intense media coverage of a number of scandals, notably those involving charities' overaggressive communications with vulnerable donors (e.g., elderly people with dementia), had caused the entire UK fundraising sector to 'step back' and reflect seriously on its seemingly widespread use of questionable practices. Thus, Hind (2017) argued that media censure of nonprofits' fundraising activities had in fact played a positive role in securing improvements in the ethicality of nonprofit organisations' fundraising methods.

Reform of fundraising practices in the UK was stimulated by the publication in 2016 of the outcomes to a government enquiry into certain high-profile fundraising scandals (House of Commons, 2016). Concurrently, and in conjunction with UK nonprofit support organisations, the UK government established a committee chaired by Sir Stuart Etherington to review the entire issue of how best to regulate fundraising practices (Etherington, 2015). The mandate of the Etherington Committee was UK-wide, although the regional governments of Scotland and Northern Ireland had the power to opt out from its consequences. Following the publication of the report, a single 'Fundraising Regulator' was set up to replace the regulatory boards of various professional organisations. This body has issued a Code of Practice on Fundraising and has taken over and consolidated the complaints procedures of all professional bodies in the field. Fundraising nonprofits are not legally obliged to subscribe to the Fundraising Regulator, but nearly all mainstream UK nonprofits have chosen to do so. The Code of Practice (first published in 2017) prohibits fundraisers from placing undue pressures on individuals to donate; from generating donations out of guilt or embarrassment; and from sending communications that are grossly indecent, offensive, or intended to cause distress or anxiety. Also, organisations must take full responsibility for the behaviour of any and all professional fundraising agencies that they employ. The Code was updated in 2021. Changes focused on 'integrity and principles' and 'diversity'. However, the updates did not materially affect any pre-existing standards. Recommendations on changes to the Code are made by the standards committee of the Fundraising Regulator.

The general topic of complaints about fundraisers was investigated by Sargeant, Hudson, and Wilson (2012), who analysed 1,349 complaints received by the Fundraising Standards Board (a body later taken over by the Fundraising Regulator) during a particular year. Face-to-face fundraising (especially doorstep solicitations undertaken by paid external agencies) had the highest number of complaints, followed by complaints about the frequency and content of direct mail, and then by telephone calls from charities. Solicitations typically generated one complaint per 1,000 approaches. Sargeant et al. (2012) argued that complaints about charities should not necessarily be seen in a negative light because charities should, as a matter of course, challenge the public and, if necessary, make people feel uncomfortable. Complaints provided feedback that, Sargeant et al. (2012) continued, could subsequently be used to improve a nonprofit's fundraising processes. More research was needed into the *positive* aspects of complaints procedures, Sargeant et al. (2012) concluded.

The prevalence (or otherwise) of the existence among UK charities of procedures for dealing with complaints from charities' beneficiaries (rather than from members of the public) was explored by Bennett and Savani (2011) who surveyed 251 human service charities to establish how many of them operated formal processes. This study also examined the determinants of (i) decisions to implement complaints procedures and (ii) whether an organisation applied a strategic approach when handling complaints. It emerged that 17% of the sample organisations (mainly small charities) had no formal complaints procedures. Factors that significantly affected the likelihood that a charity would operate a formal complaints system were an organisation's size, the percentage of its income derived from government sources, and its level of 'learning orientation'. Significant influences on whether a strategic approach would be adopted when managing complaints were a charity's beneficiary orientation, learning and listening orientations, the ease with which a beneficiary

---

Box 1.4   Research opportunities: regulatory frameworks

Little academic research has been undertaken in the charity regulation area. However, the sparsity of prior research into nonprofit regulation provides rich opportunities for original and valuable investigations. A starting point for fresh research into these matters could be the use of the UK's consolidated self-regulatory framework as a benchmark for international comparisons of regulatory regimes. In contrast to the UK system, some countries (China and a number of Middle Eastern nations for example) operate tight legal control over the activities of nonprofit organisations. Nonprofits in the USA are subject to Federal laws that apply equally to nonprofits and commercial organisations. US nonprofits may additionally be required to register with separate States, which may or may not have specific Charitable Solicitation Laws. In Canada, regulatory authority is split between Federal and Provincial governments. A Canadian nonprofit must by law spend a minimum percentage of its revenues on its 'purpose'.

A cross-national, cross-cultural study of similarities and differences among the regulatory systems of various countries would be useful. Further topics relating to the regulation of the nonprofit sector worthy of future research are (i) the sources of the views and perceptions of the journalists who periodically denounce nonprofits' fundraising activities, (ii) the opinions of charity beneficiaries regarding mass media criticisms of nonprofit fundraising practices, and (iii) nonprofit managers' interpretations of the meanings of key words and phrases in the codes of practice that exist to regulate nonprofit organisations (e.g., the meanings of the terms 'non-intimidatory approach' and 'public benefit').

could seek help from an alternative charity, and the degrees of beneficiaries' dependence on the services provided by a charity.

Commercialisation of nonprofit organisations

The remaining criticisms of nonprofit marketing covered by the present chapter concern allegations that many contemporary nonprofits are 'over-commercialised' and, in consequence, have lost sight of their original missions. Accusations of this nature challenge the proposition that nonprofit marketing is a socially valuable activity. Conversely, advocates of commercial approaches have insisted that nonprofits have much to gain in terms of efficiency, effectiveness, and the provision of superior services to beneficiaries by adopting outlooks and practices similar to those found in the for-profit sector. An upsurge of academic interest in this matter occurred during the early and mid-1960s; a period when (i) countries involved in the Second World War had recovered economically from the effects of that war, (ii) restrictions on domestic and international trade had been relaxed, and (iii) mass advertising in conjunction with the mass production of consumer goods and the ready availability of consumer credit had begun to create the 'consumer society'. A highly influential publication appearing at the time and advocating nonprofit marketing was authored by Kotler and Levy (1969), who asserted that since nonprofits 'perform marketing-like activities whether or not they are recognised as such' (p.11), they should develop marketing competencies and engage in marketing activities comparable to those of commercial businesses. This seminal article, together with other contributions expressing similar sentiments (e.g., Shapiro, 1973; Lovelock and Weinberg, 1978), engendered much comment and debate (ongoing to the present day) about the propriety and effectiveness of the infusion of 'commercial' principles into nonprofit organisations.

Researchers who have investigated the issue have noted that many of the early advocates of the application of business methods and models to nonprofit organisations were people who supported, implicitly or explicitly, neo-liberal free market approaches to economics and social organisation. Also, according to Novatorov (2018), the views of Kotler and others were inspired by exchange theory (see Chapter 2). Those who mistrust the application of commercial approaches to nonprofit marketing have questioned the usefulness of competitive behaviour (accompanied by the recruitment of nonprofit managers on the basis of their exhibiting high competitive spirit) within the helping and caring arena, suggesting that it can lead to excessive risk taking, mission drift (see below), and the use of morally dubious marketing methods and advertising techniques (see Chapter 3).

In a thoughtful conceptual paper relating to these matters, Novatorov (2014) argued that the preponderance of free-marketeers allegedly present among the academics who analysed and discussed nonprofit marketing issues at the time the subject was introduced could have exerted a restraining influence on the consideration of *collectivist* nonprofit marketing policies and practices. Collectivist approaches might, Novatorov (2014) proposed, offer a better fit with the core values and missions of most nonprofits. A collectivist approach to marketing could involve nonprofits combining their marketing efforts, cross-promoting their services, sharing resources, jointly lobbying government vis-à-vis nonprofit sector problems, collectively undertaking research into donor behaviour, and so on. The emphasis would be on co-operation among organisations rather than competition and on organisations working together to encourage people to donate. Cooperative lobbying can also involve joint efforts by nonprofit and for-profit organisations working together.

Wymer (2013) raised the question of whether free market thinking had resulted in a large number of studies of the nonprofit marketing function, reflecting a rather one-sided perception that nonprofit marketing was a quintessentially *business* function. If a nonprofit was to be run as a business, Wymer (2013) commented, the organisation's performance was likely to be evaluated using metrics copied from the for-profit sector, and those metrics might not be the best to employ. Research has not followed up these atypical ideas regarding nonprofit marketing and fundraising. So far, moreover, the 'critical marketing' research literature has not explored extensively and in-depth the application of critical theory to marketing within the nonprofit domain (see Tadajewski and Brownlie (2009) and Novatorov (2018) for accounts of the nature of critical marketing). Novatorov (2018) argued that critical thinking in this area could create many openings for valuable research.

Cowan and Hardy (2022) noted the general lack of empirical evidence about the impact of the increasing commercialisation of charities on their operations, given what the authors regarded as a shift towards 'an entrepreneurial, contract, business-related culture, which mirrors the private sector in many ways' (p. 4). They conducted a case study of the Canal and River Trust, a charity set up by the government to manage and control 2,000 miles of inland waterways in England and Wales. Interviews were completed with households who live on boats and continuously cruise on canals. Cowan and Hardy (2022) concluded that the interests of boat households had been marginalised as the charity re-shaped itself due to its reliance on government and other funding bodies. The organisation had reconfigured its thoughts about its role and activities, leading to beneficiaries such as people in boat households feeling ignored and that their interests had been deprioritised and defunded. An interesting observation arising from the study was the limit of the Charity Regulator's ability to oversee developments emerging from the growing commercialisation of the nonprofit sector.

Box 1.5   Research opportunities: cooperative nonprofit marketing

Without doubt, there is much scope for the completion of studies that contribute to the 'commercial versus collective' marketing debate through the investigation of, for example, possibilities for 'co-opetition' among nonprofits (i.e., co-operation among competing organisations); barriers to 'fair' competition in the fundraising market; and whether competitive pressures impel fundraising organisations to structure their activities in unethical manners. Conceptual as well as empirical contributions could examine whether contemporary fundraising markets are ideologically neutral. Studies of this nature must, of course, take into account the realities of the needs of nonprofit organisations to raise money to finance their operations.

Market orientation and its application to fundraising nonprofits

Research into the adoption by nonprofits of constructs borrowed from the for-profit marketing literature has largely involved studies undertaken into nonprofit organisations' levels of 'market orientation'. The term 'market orientation' refers to the extent to which an organisation applies the 'marketing concept' when completing its work. The marketing concept is the philosophy that organisations should discover and analyse customers' (donors') needs, desires, and requirements and should then take decisions in order to satisfy donors' desires and needs. Adoption of a market orientation by a fundraising nonprofit implies that it applies an essentially *business* model to its operations (see Sargeant, Foreman, and Liao, 2002; Chad, Kyriazis, and Motion, 2013). Also, nonprofits with high degrees of market orientation will be prepared to react quickly and comprehensively to changes in donors' wants and opinions.

As it has developed within the for-profit domain, the concept of market orientation has been described both as a set of processes (Kohli and Jaworski, 1990) and as a *culture* within an organisation that gives rise to specific activities (notably competitor analysis and marketing intelligence generation) (Narver and Slater, 1990). Much of the nonprofit research undertaken with respect to market orientation has sought both to (i) extend commercial notions of market orientation to the nonprofit area and (ii) measure the effects of the adoption of market orientation on fundraising performance. Research relating to nonprofit marketing orientation has been voluminous (for details, see the reviews of, for example, Liao, Foreman, and Sargeant, 2001; Shoham, Ruvio, Gadot, and Schwabsky, 2006; Duque-Zuluaga and Schneider, 2008; Modi and Mishra, 2010), although interest in the topic seems to have waned in recent years. This is due perhaps to nonprofit market orientation investigations often comprising offshoots of studies of the subject appearing in the for-profit marketing literature. Increasingly, market orientation is taken as a 'given' determinant of superior performance in the commercial sector.

To apply the market orientation concept to the nonprofit sector, Liao et al. (2001) used the term 'societal orientation' rather than 'market orientation' to describe the authors' adaptation of constructs derived from for-profit market orientation studies. This change in nomenclature, the authors suggested, helped to eliminate the 'focus on markets that for some categories of nonprofit can have little or no meaning' (p.260). Societal orientation, Liao et al. (2001) continued, included (multiple) stakeholder orientation, competitor orientation, the search for collaborations designed to acquire resources or to provide services, and inter-functional coordination of marketing issues within a nonprofit organisation. A later empirical study undertaken by Duque-Zuluaga and Schneider (2008) concluded that societal orientation comprised five sets of activities, respectively, concerning beneficiaries, donors, volunteers, employees, and collaborations with other nonprofits. Beneficiary activities involved identifying and understanding beneficiaries' needs and developing programmes to satisfy those needs. Donor-related activities were associated with the attraction of financial resources, with volunteer and employee activities, and collaborative activities to do with the establishment of partnerships and co-operations to improve donor service delivery. Performance resulting from the implementation of societal orientation, Duque-Zuluaga and Schneider (2008) continued, should be assessed in terms of total value of donations, the expenses to donor–income ratio, the number of new donors attracted, the value of government grants obtained, and the number of 'major' gifts from individuals and foundations. Wymer et al. (2015) contributed to this line of research via a study that developed a construct which the authors labelled 'nonprofit market orientation'. This construct comprised four component orientations: nonprofit brand orientation, supporter, commercial, and service orientations. While discussing the development of their scale, Wymer et al. (2015) noted how most of the scales that had been employed to measure the market orientation construct in nonprofit settings were themselves based on scales created and applied within the commercial sector. This may have meant, Wymer et al. (2015) commented, that commercial assumptions influenced the researchers who created market orientation inventories for the nonprofit sector.

Taken in the round, studies have suggested that the financial effects of the adoption of market orientation by nonprofits have been positive (see Shoham et al.'s [2006] meta-analysis of investigations relating to this matter and also the critical reflections on nonprofit market orientation offered by Wymer, Boenigk, and Mohlmann [2015]). It is relevant to note, however, that few of these studies considered the effects of a nonprofit's marketing orientation on its beneficiaries. The idea of *beneficiary orientation* was introduced by Bennett (2005) and extended by Modi and Mishra (2010). The latter study defined beneficiary orientation as an 'organisational focus on understanding the explicit and latent needs of beneficiaries, designing services to meet those needs, and regularly monitoring beneficiary satisfaction' (p.554). Bennett's earlier (2005) study of 172 UK charities found that organisations that were market orientated vis-à-vis fundraising were also market orientated when marketing their services to beneficiaries. Antecedents of beneficiary market orientation identified by Bennett's (2005) study included the extent of competition among nonprofits operating in the same field, the volume of the supply of beneficiaries, and the presence of innately competitive instincts among a charity's senior managers.

Mission drift and its detractors

A common criticism of the adoption of market orientation by fundraising non-profits is its alleged tendency to lead to mission drift (sometimes referred to as mission creep). Mission drift occurs when a nonprofit raises a substantial part of its income (sometimes most of its income) through working for commercial businesses or (more usually) for government agencies under commercial contracts. The practice of nonprofit organisations bidding for government contract work is today a common feature of the fundraising scene in the UK and the USA and is spreading to other countries. The main objection to a nonprofit undertaking contract work is that the nonprofit's priorities and activities might come to be largely determined by an external funder and not by the nonprofit. Commonly, the main external funder is a central or local government agency that issues contracts to nonprofits to supply human welfare or environmental protection services (usually services that in the past the state itself would provide). Sometimes, the outside funder occupies seats on the nonprofit's governing board and hence plays a 'hands-on role' in determining the organisation's vision and mission statements. This might occur most often among nonprofits that find it difficult to attract and retain board members. Government contracting to nonprofits is especially common in relation to healthcare and is increasingly employed in fields such as road safety, prisoner rehabilitation, child protection, and the provision of social housing.

Mission drift has, in the words of Ebrahim, Battilanna, and Mair (2014 p.82), become a 'profound trend' during the last 40 years as governments have withdrawn from social services provision. Most research in the area has regarded mission drift as improper and harmful and has recommended various methods for avoiding its occurrence. A primary source of negative opinion regarding mission drift was a paper by Weisbrod (2004), which accused mission drift of diverting time, energy, and money away from an affected nonprofit's mission, of leading the nonprofit to compete against private providers for government contracts and, in consequence, of fomenting competitive commercial instincts among the managers of nonprofit organisations. Donors would become reluctant to give money to the nonprofit in question as they would not believe that the organisation was fulfilling its original mission. Hence, Weisbrod (2004) argued, nonprofits should avoid all activities not directly related to their core philanthropic aims.

This theme was subsequently pursued by a number of authors including, for example, Cornforth (2014), who applied Institutional Theory to analyse the issue. (Institutional Theory in this context examines how organisational structures, rules, norms, and routines become established as authoritative guidelines for behaviour.) Mission drift could be combatted, Cornforth (2014) suggested, by (i) imposing a legal structure on a nonprofit to separate contract work from the organisation's normal operations, (ii) compartmentalising government or commercial contract activities, (iii) ensuring that all the nonprofit's board of trustees were opposed to mission drift, and (iv) selecting employees who also disliked mission drift. Ebrahim et al. (2014) likewise contended that nonprofits should apply different legal and governance structures to their non-core projects since otherwise an organisation's priorities could shift away from its philanthropic aims. It was important, Ebrahim et al. (2014) concluded, that a nonprofit not become more accountable to government agencies than to its trustees and beneficiaries. This possibility was investigated directly by Henderson and Lambert (2018) who, in the course of four case studies of Scottish charities, observed how a nonprofit's management accounting information systems was likely to alter after the receipt of large government contracts. The funder would stipulate specific accounting procedures, would shape performance measures, and would require bespoke reporting and accountability mechanisms that influenced decision-making within a charity.

Noting that mission drift could create internal tensions within a fundraising nonprofit and additionally that it might create a lack of support from critical stakeholders, Ramus and Vaccaro (2017) suggested that mission drift could be avoided if all of a nonprofit's stakeholders insisted on becoming deeply engaged in all aspects of the organisation's decision-making. The authors completed two case studies, the outcomes to which demonstrated that dialogue with stakeholders vis-à-vis a nonprofit's strategies and objectives was an effective tool for averting mission drift. Stakeholder engagement was just as effective a means for obviating mission drift, Ramus and Vaccaro (2017) opined, as were organisational design, employee interventions, or the application of accounting tools designed to preserve a nonprofit's beneficiary orientation. Tensions arising between a nonprofit's social mission and the requirement that it meet the demands of a market economy were investigated by Sanders (2015) who, through an ethnographic study of a single case nonprofit organisation, found that the 'mission/market' dilemma within the nonprofit was managed in both a contradictory *and* an interconnected manner. Specific and disparate forms of internal communication arose to support relationships between these seemingly incompatible goals.

An interesting survey of 521 Swiss nonprofit organisations undertaken by Hersberger-Langloh, Stühlinger, and von Schnurbein (2020) explored the consequences of mimetic, normative, and coercive pressures on tendencies towards mission drift. The authors noted how the institutionalisation of business-like practices in recent decades had resulted in nonprofits increasingly looking alike. Three mechanisms were said to contribute to this outcome: coercive, mimetic, and normative isomorphism. Coercive isomorphism resulted from political and regulatory influences, mimetic isomorphism was a response to uncertainty, and normative isomorphism was brought about by pressures arising from the influence of managers with professional nonprofit management experience. Findings indicated that normative pressures had a negative indirect effect on mission drift, but that neither mimetic pressure nor internal management exerted direct effects. Coercive pressure had a positive direct effect on mission drift, which could take place without an organisation having strategies or internal processes in place.

Notwithstanding the widespread negative opinion about mission drift expressed in much of the literature on the subject, three case studies of UK charities completed by Bennett (2011) found that all three of the organisations investigated accepted mission drift as a fact of life and, instead of merely carrying out government contracts, sought to initiate projects and to direct, control, and assume strategic responsibility for state-funded projects. The three charities were highly proactive in their dealings with state agencies. For example, the charities offered to train personnel from state agencies in matters relating to a charity's work, furnished consultancy services, proposed ideas for fresh joint projects, and suggested targets and performance criteria. This proactivity turned a charity's government contract activities to the charity's advantage.

References

Allred, A. and Amos, C. (2023) "A Processing Fluency Perspective on Overhead Aversion: How Much is Too Much?", *Journal of Philanthropy and Marketing*, Early View, 1–17.

Bennett, R. (2005) "Competitive Environment, Market Orientation, and the Use of Relational Approaches to the Marketing of Beneficiary Services", *Journal of Services Marketing* 19 (7), 453–469.

Bennett, R. (2011) "Surviving Mission Drift: How Charities Can Turn Dependence on Government Contract Funding to Their Own Advantage", *Nonprofit Management and Leadership* 22 (2), 217–231.

Bennett, R. (2013a) "Factors Influencing the Break-Even Probabilities of Agency Recruited Low Value Charity Donors", *Voluntas* 24 (4), 1091–1112.

Bennett, R. (2013b) "Factors Influencing the Probability of Early Lapse of Face to Face Recruited Charity Donors", *International Review on Public and Nonprofit Marketing* 10 (2), 129–142.

Bennett, R. and Savani, S. (2003) "Predicting the Accuracy of Public Perceptions of Charity Performance", *Journal of Targeting, Measurement and Analysis for Marketing* 11 (4), 326–342.

Bennett, R. and Savani, S. (2011) "Complaints Handling Procedures of Human Services Charities: Prevalence, Antecedents and Strategic Approaches", *Managing Service Quality: An International Journal* 21 (5), 484–510.

Chad, P., Kyriazis, E. and Motion, J. (2013) "Development of a Market Orientation Research Agenda for the Nonprofit Sector", *Journal of Nonprofit and Public Sector Marketing* 25 (1), 1–27.

Cornforth, C. (2014) "Understanding and Combating Mission Drift in Social Enterprises", *Social Enterprise Journal* 10 (1), 3–20.

Cowan, D. and Hardy, B. (2022) "Charitable Purposes and the Shaping Effects of Money", *International Journal of Law in Context*, Early view, 1–16.

Dean, J. and Wood, R. (2017) "You Can Try to Press Different Emotional Buttons: The Conflicts and Strategies of Eliciting Emotions for Fundraisers", *International Journal of Nonprofit and Voluntary Sector Marketing* 22 (4), e1603.

Duque-Zuluaga, L. and Schneider, V. (2008) "Market Orientation and Organisational Performance in the Nonprofit Context: Exploring Both Concepts and the Relationships Between Them", *Journal of Nonprofit and Public Sector Marketing* 19 (2), 25–49.

Ebrahim, A., Battilanna, J. and Mair, J. (2014) "The Governance of Social Enterprises: Mission Drift and Accountability Challenges in Hybrid Organisations", *Research in Organisational Behaviour* 34, 81–100.

Etherington, S. (2015) *Regulating Fundraising for the Future: Trust in Charities, Confidence in Fundraising Regulation*, London: National Council for Voluntary Organisations. Accessed at vcvo.org.uk.

Gies, L. (2021) "Charity Fundraising and the Ethics of Voice: Cancer Survivors' Perspectives on Macmillan Cancer Support's 'Brave the Shave' Campaign", *Journal of Media Ethics* 36 (2), 85–96.

Henderson, E. and Lambert, V. (2018) "Negotiating for Survival: Balancing Mission and Money", *British Accounting Review* 50 (2), 185–198.

Hersberger-Langloh, S., Stühlinger, S. and von Schnurbein, G. (2020) "Institutional Isomorphism and Nonprofit Managerialism: For Better or Worse?", *Nonprofit Management and Leadership* 31 (3), 461–480.

Hind, A. (2017) "New Development: Fundraising in UK Charities – Stepping Back from the Abyss", *Public Money and Management* 37 (3), 205–210.

House of Commons. (2016) *The 2015 Charity Fundraising Controversy: Lessons for Trustees, the Charity Commission, and Regulators*, London: House of Commons Public Administration and Constitutional Committee. Accessed at www.publicationsparliament.uk.

Kohli, A. and Jaworski, B. (1990) "Market Orientation: The Construct, Research Propositions and Managerial Implications", *Journal of Marketing* 54 (2), 1–18.

Kotler, P. and Levy, S. (1969) "Broadening the Concept of Marketing", *Journal of Marketing* 33 (1), 10–15.

Lee, Y. (2021) "Nonprofit Marketing Expenses: Who Spends More than Others?", *Journal of Nonprofit and Public Sector Marketing* 33 (3), 385–402.

Liao, M., Foreman, S. and Sargeant, A. (2001) "Market versus Societal Orientation in the Nonprofit Context", *International Journal of Nonprofit and Voluntary Sector Marketing* 6 (3), 254–268.

Lovelock, C. and Weinberg, C. (1978) *Public and Nonprofit Marketing Comes of Age*, Stanford CA: Graduate School of Business Stanford University

MacQuillin, I. (2016) *Rights Stuff: Fundraising's Ethics Gap and a New Normative Theory of Fundraising Ethics*, Plymouth: Centre for Sustainable Philanthropy, Plymouth University.

MacQuillin, I. (2022) "Normative Fundraising Ethics: A Review of the Field", *Journal of Philanthropy and Marketing*, e1740.

Modi, P. and Mishra, D. (2010) "Conceptualising Market Orientation in Nonprofit Organisations: Definition, Performance, and Preliminary Construction of a Scale", *Journal of Marketing Management* 26 (5/6), 548–569.

Narver, J. and Slater, S. (1990) "The Effect of a Market Orientation on Business Philosophy", *Journal of Marketing* 54 (3), 20–35.

Newman, G., Shniderman, A., Cain, D. and Sevel, K. (2019) "Do the Ends Justify the Means? The Relative Focus on Overhead Versus Outcomes in Charitable Fundraising", *Nonprofit and Voluntary Sector Quarterly* 48 (1), 71–90.

Novatorov, E. (2014) "Nonprofit Marketing: Theory Triangulation", *SSRN Paper* https://ssrn.com/abstract=2515224.

Novatorov, E. (2018) "Toward Improving the Quality of Empirical Public and Nonprofit Research: Advocating for a Pluralistic Methodological Approach", *International Review on Public and Nonprofit Marketing* 15 (1), 67–86.

Qu, H. and Daniel, J. (2021) "Is 'Overhead' A Tainted Word? A Survey Experiment Exploring Framing Effects of Nonprofit Overhead on Donor Decision", *Nonprofit and Voluntary Sector Quarterly* 50 (2), 397–419.

Ramus, T. and Vaccaro, A. (2017) "Stakeholders Matter: How Social Enterprises Address Mission Drift", *Journal of Business Ethics* 143 (2), 307–322.

Rau, H., Samek, A. and Zhurakhovska, L. (2022) "Do I Care If You Are Paid? Field Experiments and Expert Forecasts in Charitable Giving", *Journal of Economic Behaviour and Organisation* 195, 42–51.

Sanders, M. (2015) "Being Nonprofit Like in a Market Economy: Understanding the Mission-Market Tension in Nonprofit Organising", *Nonprofit and Voluntary Sector Quarterly* 44 (2), 205–222.

Sargeant, A., Ford, J. and West, D. (2000) "Widening the Appeal of Charity", *International Journal of Non-profit and Voluntary Sector Marketing* 5 (4), 318–332.

Sargeant, A., Foreman, S. and Liao, M (2002) "Operationalising the Marketing Concept in the Nonprofit Sector", *Journal of Nonprofit and Public Sector Marketing* 10 (2), 41–65.

Sargeant, A., Hudson, J. and Wilson, S. (2012) "Donor Complaints About Fundraising: What Are They and Why Should We Care?", *Voluntas* 23 (3), 791–807.

Sargeant, A., Lee, S. and Jay, E. (2009) "Communicating the 'Realities' of Charity Costs: An Institute of Fundraising Initiative", *Nonprofit and Voluntary Sector Quarterly* 38 (2), 333–342.

Schubert, P. and Boenigk, S. (2019) "The Nonprofit Starvation Cycle: Empirical Evidence from a German Context", *Nonprofit and Voluntary Sector Quarterly* 48 (3), 467–491.

Shapiro, B. (1973) "Marketing for Nonprofits", *Harvard Business Review*, September–October 1973, 123–132.

Shoham, A., Ruvio, A., Gadot, E. and Schwabsky, N. (2006) "Market Orientations in the Nonprofit and Voluntary Sector: A Meta-analysis of their Relationships with Organisational Performance", *Nonprofit and Voluntary Sector Quarterly* 35 (3), 453–476.

Tadajewski, M. and Brownlie, D. (2009) *Critical Marketing: Issues in Contemporary Marketing*, London: Wiley.

Waldner, C., Willems, J., Ehmann, J. and Gies, F. (2020) "The Impact of Face-to-Face Street Fundraising on Organisational Reputation", *International Journal of Nonprofit and Voluntary Sector Marketing*, 25 (4), e1672.

Weisbrod, B. (2004) "The Pitfalls if Profit", *Stanford Social Innovation Review* 2 (3), 40–47.

Wymer, W. (2013) "The Influence of Marketing Scholarship's Legacy on Nonprofit Marketing", *International Journal of Financial Studies* 1 (3), 102–118.

Wymer, W., Boenigk, S. and Mohlmann, M. (2015) "The Conceptualisation of Nonprofit Market Orientation: A Critical Reflection and Contributions Toward Closing the Practice-Theory Gap", *Journal of Nonprofit and Public Sector Marketing* 27 (2), 117–134.

2 Frameworks and foundations

Giving to nonprofits is known to have occurred as far back as written records concerning the matter are available. Evidence of philanthropic free-of-charge healthcare facilities that operated in the third century BC has been found in Egypt, Sri Lanka, and India. Wealthy individuals in Ancient Greece sponsored sports events and food distributions to the poor. Philanthropic giving was common in Ancient Rome, where high-value donors received much public acclaim (see Block [2000] for a history of the nonprofit sectors of various countries). The current chapter examines research that attempted (i) to explain why people donate to charitable causes, (ii) to identify 'the giving type' of individual, (iii) to develop predictive models of giving, and (iv) to determine the factors that induce people to donate to particular genres of cause. Giving by businesses is also covered by the chapter, including research into the motives that induce corporate philanthropy, cause-related marketing (CRM), and company sponsorship of nonprofit organisations.

Giving by individuals

Many of the early theories of why individual people are motivated to donate to fundraising nonprofits were inspired by Social Exchange Theory (Homans, 1958). When applied to fundraising, Social Exchange Theory asserts that relations between a nonprofit and its donors comprise a series of exchanges and interactions that create reciprocal obligations. Social Exchange Theory assumes that *feelings* constitute exchangeable resources. Thus, a person may donate money or time to a nonprofit and in return obtains positive feelings and emotions of, for example, satisfaction, self-esteem, and personal well-being. Giving to a nonprofit, according to this view, offers the donor 'expressive benefits', i.e., opportunities to express personal values and to reinforce the individual's self-identity as a philanthropic person. Exchange theory assumes that donors are rational and calculate the costs and (emotional) benefits of making a gift. A donation occurs if the latter outweighs the former.

Critics of the theory point to its (allegedly excessive) focus on the individual rather than on social or cultural influences and to the supposition

DOI: 10.4324/9781003364405-2

that people *selfishly* seek need fulfilment. Cropanzano and Mitchell (2005) published a valuable interdisciplinary review of theories and literature relating to Social Exchange Theory and disparaged the theory on a number of grounds additional to those previously mentioned. For example, the core ideas underlying Exchange Theory had yet to be fully identified and articulated, Cropanzano and Mitchell (2005) opined, and the theory lacked a unifying framework. A significant drawback of Social Exchange Theory, the authors continued, was that it offered only a partial explanation of pro-social behaviour, given that in reality many variables other than exchange reciprocity affect donation decisions. Also, empirical tests of the theory had tended to ignore crucial influences on giving. Exchanges of money for feelings of personal satisfaction rarely involve *explicit* bargains, the authors suggested, and the emotional resources exchanged in return for a donation are ambiguous and difficult to measure. Hence, Cropanzano and Mitchell (2005) concluded, complete and integrated model specifications were needed prior to attempts to estimate models based on Social Exchange Theory.

Today, Social Exchange Theory is employed more commonly perhaps to underpin studies appearing in the social marketing literature than in the nonprofit fundraising field. Nevertheless, some interest in Social Exchange Theory persists within the nonprofit and fundraising domain, as evidenced by research papers authored by, for example, Schindler, Reinhard, Stahlberg, and Len (2014); Ye, Teng, Yu, and Wang (2015); and Zhao, Chen, Wang, and Chen (2017). The first of these papers involved an empirical study that employed an adaptation of a pre-existing 'exchange orientation scale' to assess the effects of high exchange orientation on the nonprofit donation intention of 67 university students. (Allegedly, a person with high exchange orientation will track and mentally 'keep scores' of obligations and is likely to want rapid reciprocation.) Specifically, the authors queried whether individuals with high exchange orientation were less likely to give than people with minimal exchange orientation. Lower amounts of giving were anticipated from high exchange orientation people because it was assumed that study participants who possessed high exchange orientation would expect immediate and substantial rewards that they perceived to be at least comparable with their assessments of the worth of their financial sacrifice. Realisation of this expectation was necessary in order that a high exchange orientation person could establish 'exchange equality' following a donation. However, expectations might be unrealistic and often would not be met. Findings from the investigation indicated that it was in fact the case that the probability that a person would donate decreased as exchange orientation increased (at least among the members of this small sample). The authors attributed the results to high exchange orientation people experiencing greater feelings of exchange inequality consequent to making a gift.

Ye et al. (2015) completed another study that drew on Social Exchange Theory (again based on a relatively small sample of undergraduate students) and which argued that charity appeals which focused on 'benefits to self', i.e., appeals that were aimed at ego-enhancement, self-esteem, etc., were likely to generate greater donation intentions whenever the appeals were framed in 'individualistic' cultural contexts. To test this assertion, the authors conducted experiments in Canada (an individualistic country) and in China, where collectivist cultures prevail. In each country, two versions of a scenario containing an appeal (one framed individualistically and the other framed collectivistically) were administered to the students (58 in China and 49 in Canada). The results suggested that charitable appeals framed around benefits to self were positively associated with higher donation intentions when the appeals were used in individualistic cultural contexts. The findings also indicated that people of high social status exhibited greater donation intention when viewing appeals directed at 'self'.

Zhao et al.'s (2017) study used Social Exchange Theory as the foundation of an investigation of 204 people known to participate in crowdfunding (see Chapter 4). The authors observed that nonprofit crowdfunding appeals were generally more successful than commercial crowdfunding solicitations. This was due, Zhao et al. (2017) suggested, to the possibility that donors to nonprofit crowdfunded projects received rewards for their gifts in terms of feelings of gratification, of experiencing a sense of belonging, of having an outlet to express sympathy for a cause, and through being able to make friends with other donors. A structural equation model was constructed to explain the study participants' donation intentions. Findings from a test of the model indicated that donation intention depended significantly on the attractiveness of a project (which gave rise to 'commitment') and that the strength of the impact of commitment on donation intention was significantly influenced by participants' levels of trust in the competence of the management of the soliciting organisation. The authors suggested that the results of the investigation were consistent with Social Exchange Theory because (according to Homans [1958]) commitment and trust lie at the heart of a person's willingness to enter into an exchange relationship.

Box 2.1   Research opportunities: Social Exchange Theory

Social Exchange Theory has been used in attempts to reveal the underlying forces that drive giving decisions. It offers a basic framework for understanding donation behaviour and indeed for analysing social behaviour in general. It is clear, nevertheless, that the theory is contentious and problematic, thus creating opportunities for fresh and creative research. One set of research opportunities relevant to Social Exchange Theory arises from Cropanzano and Mitchell's (2005) observation that people have different 'reciprocity norms'. What specifically are these reciprocity norms and how do they vary with respect to disparate types of people and to various forms of fundraising? What are the antecedents of particular categories of feelings of satisfaction when people make gifts? Do emotional responses change over time; do they differ according to the size, image, and reputation of a nonprofit? Does a donor's opinion of the importance to the nonprofit of the person's gift affect the individual's feelings and emotions when making the gift?

One school of thought relating to Exchange Theory relies on the principles of reinforcement found in Skinnerian operant psychology (see Emerson [1976] for details of this matter and for a wide-ranging critique of Social Exchange Theory). To establish *which* reinforcements are relevant within charity giving scenarios, it would be necessary to undertake in-depth studies of individual donors over time and within bounded environments hence enabling researchers to manipulate sequentially different stimulus conditions. Homans (1974) was an early advocate of the Skinnerian operant conditioning approach, proposing that (i) the greater the frequency with which a particular action of a person is rewarded, the more likely the person is to perform that action, and (ii) (the 'deprivation–satiation hypothesis') the 'more often in the recent past a person has received a particular reward, the *less* valuable any further unit of that reward becomes for that individual' (p. 29). Both of these propositions are testable in the fundraising context, especially vis-à-vis relationship marketing (see Chapter 3).

Warm glow and its influence on giving

The relevance of a donor's feelings as a form of reciprocity when making a gift has been known to fundraisers for many years and has given rise to many of the fundraising practices covered by this and other chapters of the book. A major form of emotional reward for giving that might be received by donors is a 'warm glow' (often referred to as 'helper's high') experienced when making a donation. Warm glow is the pleasurable emotion that results from helping a deserving cause. Allegedly, warm glow leads to feelings of calmness, inner self-worth, and physical warmth. It is sometimes regarded as a 'selfish' motive for making a gift (see below), in that the donor may expect a warm glow as a reward for making a gift and be driven to donate through desiring a warm glow experience. Whatever its source, warm glow has been found to underlie nonprofit donation behaviour in many situations.

A seminal study undertaken by Williamson and Clark (1989) found that warm glow constituted an extremely strong motive for pro-social behaviour in certain individuals. A predisposition to experience warm glow, Williamson and Clarke (1989) concluded, was associated with psychologically selfish reasons for giving, as it made donors feel more positively about themselves. For some people therefore, the act of donating was little more than a mercenary and egoistical device for improving the giver's internal sense of well-being. According to this interpretation, giving to a nonprofit provides people with opportunities to assert inwardly that they are 'good' individuals with high ideals and sound moral values. This in turn supposedly results in surges of self-gratifying positive emotion, leading to generous and frequent donations. Experiments conducted by Bischoff and Krauskopf (2015) found that individual giving generated greater amounts of warm glow in study participants than collective giving, reinforcing the proposition that egoistic motives can represent an important determinant of donor behaviour. Carpenter (2021) tested the commonly held assumption that the warm glow experienced by donors is concave in nature, i.e., that it diminishes as donations grow. This made sense, Carpenter (2021) argued, because otherwise donors would give all that they could. The author applied a variety of flexible functional forms to data obtained from a sample of 1,107 house-to-house solicitations. The results confirmed that, for participants claiming warm glow as their primary motivation to give, warm glow was indeed increasing and concave.

Andreoni (1990) authored an early and influential theoretical economics exploration of the effects of warm glow in a paper that differentiated between 'pure altruism' and 'other' emotional influences on donation behaviour, e.g., feelings of prestige, guilt, or sympathy; wanting to receive social acclaim; or 'simply a desire for warm glow' (p. 464). Referring to earlier studies on the topic, Andreoni (1990) noted the lack of predictive power of the 'pure altruism model' and concluded that donors gain positive utility (in the microeconomic sense) from the very act of giving, especially vis-à-vis warm glow. The construct of warm glow has been incorporated into numerous of empirical studies of giving behaviour. An interesting field experiment that tested Andreoni's (1990) propositions was Karlan and Wood's (2017) study of the responses of recipients of direct marketing solicitations. The solicitations sent to a sample of existing donors to a nonprofit organisation either informed, or did not inform, the participants of the outcome to an investigation into the nonprofit's effectiveness in serving its beneficiaries. When this information was provided, people who in the past had donated large amounts now gave more to the organisation, whereas small donors gave less. The authors attributed their findings to the likelihood that large donors were motivated by altruism, whereas small donors were motivated more by warm glow. According to Karlan and Wood (2017), the provision of the factual information had the effect of 'turning off' a small donor's emotional trigger for giving.

Warm glow has been considered in research relating to the issue of why wealthy people have consistently been observed to give lower percentages of their incomes to nonprofits than the poor. (This matter is discussed at length in a later Section). Having observed that human service charities comprised a large part of the fundraising nonprofit sector, Mayo and Tinsley (2009) argued

Box 2.2   Research opportunities: warm glow

A number of studies have sought to dissect the construct of warm glow experimentally in order to distinguish feelings of warm glow from those of related and/or comparable emotions. Often this is done by presenting test subjects with various options allegedly associated with differing levels of selfishness or by offering disparate hypothetical incentives for donating. Unfortunately, few generalisable outcomes have emerged from this line of research, due perhaps to the possible conflation of warm glow with other emotions and also because social desirability bias in study participants' responses could arise. Social desirability bias (i.e., the tendency of test subjects to answer questions in ways that show them in a good light) can result in test subjects understating their selfish motives for giving and overstating purely altruistic motives. Future research in the area might assess the universality (or otherwise) of warm glow across cultures and, if differences exist, could investigate the antecedents of disparities. A major issue requiring attention is the question of whether warm glow is a *cause* or an *effect* of giving. The answer to this question has many implications for fundraising. Another worthwhile area for further research would be the possible existence of differences in warm glow experienced by individuals when confronted with various solicitation methods. In particular, do 'assertive' approaches impact negatively on warm glow, and does the impact of assertive solicitations vary according to a potential donor's personality traits. Two additional suggestions for research into warm glow are (i) whether the effects of warm glow are linear or follow an inverted-U pattern and (ii) examination of the strengths of social norms on warm glow experiences, differentiated with respect to the consequences of disparate types of social influence.

in a theoretical paper that the wealthy are relatively less generous than the poor, substantially because they experience less warm glow than do the poor when contemplating the plight of the beneficiaries of human service nonprofits. The rich were prone to attribute the problems of the beneficiaries of human service charities more to the beneficiaries' lack of effort during their past lives than to circumstance and chance.

Predictive models of giving behaviour

Poor levels of predictive power on the part of the above-mentioned models prompted a number or researchers to attempt to develop more general, complete, and integrated models of philanthropic giving. Notable among these efforts were the models proposed by Bendapudi, Singh, and Bendapudi (1996) and by Sargeant (1999). Bendapudi et al. (1996) distinguished between two categories of variables that the authors believed were capable of determining helping and giving behaviour. The two categories were termed source variables and donor variables. Source variables comprised, *inter alia*, a nonprofit's image of efficiency and effectiveness, the nature of the organisation's messages, portrayals of the organisation's beneficiaries, and the way in which the nonprofit asked for contributions. Donor variables consisted of donors' motives (egoistic, altruistic, or both), mood states, self-perceptions, and social pressures. Sargeant (1999) criticised Bendapudi et al.'s (1996) model on a number of grounds. Firstly, Bendapudi et al.'s (1996) model did not, in Sargeant's (1999) view, consider the factors that donors use when choosing between the giving options made available to them. Secondly, Sargeant (1999) asserted that the model neglected the (crucial) role of a fundraising nonprofit's service quality and its mechanisms for obtaining feedback. Thirdly, the model contained too few personality trait variables that possessed the potential to influence donation behaviour. Sargeant's (1999) own model included (i) 'intrinsic' variables, e.g., a donor's need for self-esteem, values, feelings of guilt, pity, empathy, fear, and sympathy; (ii) 'extrinsic' variables, e.g., age, gender, social class, income, and location; and (iii) 'perceptions', e.g., portrayals of beneficiaries, fit with self, strength of messages, branding and reputation, and mode of ask.

Sargeant continued this line of work in collaboration with Lucy Woodliffe and offered in 2007 an extensive taxonomy of the numerous variables that might influence charitable giving (Sargeant and Woodliffe, 2007). A similar inventory of factors that possibly affect donation behaviour was prepared by Bekkers and Wiepking (2011). The latter authors reviewed 500 academic articles on charitable giving, isolating eight mechanisms that supposedly drove donation decisions, i.e., awareness of need, solicitation (the ask), financial costs and benefits of giving (tax relief, etc.), altruism, an organisation's reputation, psychological benefits (helper's high, enhanced self-esteem), the match of a person's values with those of a supported nonprofit, and an organisation's perceived efficiency and effectiveness. Bekkers and Wiepking (2011) noted, however, that while there was 'an overwhelming body of knowledge available on philanthropy in the (general) social sciences across many disciplines' (p. 924), there was hardly any crossover of this literature with practical fundraising. This lack of connection between scholarly work on philanthropy and its application to practical fundraising raised questions about the usefulness of academic research in the field. A further and useful listing of motives to donate, accompanied by a brief explanation of each motive, was included in a paper authored by Mainardes, Laurett, Degasperi, and Lasso (2016). This particular study grouped 46 potential motives under five headings: environmental or public policy related, the cause, the characteristics of the nonprofit, the influence of others, and personal reward (e.g., warm glow).

Taken as a whole, predictive models of donor behaviour have included a very large number of variables. A useful contribution to the field was a study by Kumar and Chakrabarti (2023) who identified and reviewed 148 articles on the subject published from 1980 onwards and who developed a valuable classification scheme containing numerous categories and attributes. Nevertheless, the range of possible influences offered has been so wide that is difficult to suggest how a predictive model such as those described above can be applied in practice. One way forward in this respect is the creation of parsimonious scales that measure meaningful sub-sets of potential causal factors. An example was a paper by Webb, Green, and Brashear (2000), who created a scale containing four items to measure a person's attitude towards helping others (e.g., 'people in need should receive support from others'), and five items to assess attitude regarding charitable organisations (e.g., 'charitable organisations have been quite successful in helping the needy'). Similarly, an 18-item 'motives to donate' scale was constructed by Konrath and Handy 2018) containing six dimensions: trust, altruism, social factors, tax benefits, egoism, and constraints on giving. The usefulness of scales of this nature rests on their capacity to represent in miniature the numerous factors and constructs that, for operational purposes, cannot be included in a single empirical investigation.

The 'giving type'

A primary objective of many studies of giving behaviour has been the discovery of the personal traits and sociodemographic characteristics that comprehensively profile the 'giving type' of person. Another aim of investigations into the motives behind individual giving has been the prediction of the sorts of nonprofit organisation that particular groups of people are likely to support, and the explanation of differences in levels of generosity among various donor categories. One attempt at identifying the 'giving type' of person was de Oliveira, Croson, and Eckel's (2011) series of experiments designed to isolate 'giving type' individuals among a sample of 190 (non-student) low-income (mainly Afro-American) people, each of whom was asked to donate hypothetical amounts of money to various nonprofits. The study employed demographics (age, gender, number of children, employment status, family circumstances, etc.) to segment the sample. Although none of these demographic variables correlated significantly with donation choices, there did exist among the participants a giving type, in that individuals who (hypothetically) donated generously to one charity also gave generously to others. An important practical implication of this result, the authors concluded, was that the practice of donor list trading among fundraising nonprofits was worthwhile, as the contact details of 'giving type' people could be exchanged.

A somewhat different result regarding this matter was obtained by White, Poulson, and Hyde (2016), who surveyed a sample of 203 undergraduate students about their intentions to donate money to charity. The authors hypothesised that intentions to give were determined by a person's (i) self-identity as a generally helpful person, (ii) self-identity as a donor to charity, (iii) degrees of conscientiousness and agreeableness, and (iv) variables taken from the Theory of Planned Behaviour (i.e., attitude towards donating [giving is good/bad], subjective norm [perceived pressure from others to donate], and perceived behavioural control [degree of control over when/how giving is undertaken]). Findings indicated that the significant determinants of donation intention comprised subjective norm, perceived behavioural control, and a person's self-identity as a charity donor, but *not* self-identity as a helpful person in general.

Attempts to describe a 'giving type' (and indeed investigations of the motives for giving as a whole) have usually considered the individual person as the unit of analysis. Studies of giving by households, as a collective entity, have been sparse. One such exploration of household giving, however, was that of Burgoyne, Young, and Walker (2005) who observed how interactive processes within households could exert powerful influences on donation behaviour. The authors convened six focus groups to examine the effects on personal and on joint charity donation decisions within households of (i) the levels of personal financial autonomy prevailing in a household and (ii) whether individual or joint decisions determined whether, how much, and to which organisation people in the household should give. Burgoyne et al. (2005) found that charitable giving was dealt with predominantly in accordance with the style and methods through which a household managed its money in general. If spending on physical goods, insurances, etc., and decisions on how much a household would save (and how savings were organised) were determined jointly by household members, then charity donation decisions would also be jointly determined.

Investigations into household, as opposed to individual, giving decisions should be an important concern for nonprofit academics. A helpful contribution to what (little) is known about the matter was a study of the influences of specific forms of household *structure* on giving undertaken by Denis, Pecheux, and Decrop (2018). The researchers segmented the Belgian donor market using data from the official Belgian Statistics Bureau on citizens' tax and charitable giving returns over the period from 2005 to 2012. Findings from the study showed that while household composition significantly determined donation levels, important discontinuities applied, i.e., giving patterns differed according to particular household structures, and measures of behaviour did not generate continuous variables. For instance, households with different numbers of children donated, on average, disparate amounts to charity. However, the amounts donated did not increase or decrease in a linear fashion. Discontinuities also became apparent in other variables covered by the study. An interesting aspect of this paper was the authors' critique of prior research on charity giving based on their observation that studies in the field have been mainly Anglo-Saxon in origin and have presumed that donors are isolated individuals who make donation decisions independently. The influences of social, environmental, public policy, and institutional factors were often underestimated, the authors opined.

Denis et al.'s (2018) study could be followed up in a number of directions. The influence of Anglo-Saxon research norms and cultures on the configurations of models of donor behaviour and on the assumptions included in such models is clearly worthy of further investigation. Also, the discontinuities noted in Denis et al.'s (2018) work merit additional and detailed analysis. Comprehensive and integrated models of household (as opposed to individual) charity giving are needed and could be tested across different national cultures.

Donors' choices of causes and nonprofits

Why, for example, do some people opt to give to a home for stray cats whereas others choose to donate to cancer research? A study completed by Bennett (2003) tackled this question via a survey of 250 members of the general public in London. The participants were given a hypothetical sum of money and asked to donate the entire amount to one of three nonprofits, each dealing with a different genre of cause (cancer, animal welfare, human rights). It emerged that similarities between an individual's personal values and a nonprofit organisation's values significantly affected a donor's choice of cause. Also, 'individualistic' people were more likely to select the human rights nonprofit, whereas 'empathetic' participants were more likely to choose the cancer or the animal welfare charities. Another study that focused on donors' personal values in relation to the choice of a charity to support was undertaken by Sneddon, Evers, and Lee (2020) who examined the effects of people's 'value priorities' on selections. Differences in the priority given to various personal values by samples of donors in Australia and the United States were investigated in relation to support for nine different types of charitable cause. It emerged that disparities in value priorities significantly affected decisions to support particular genres of cause.

A valuable contribution to research on the issue of charity choice was Wiepking's (2010) analysis of the responses of 1,246 participants to the 'Giving in the Netherlands Panel Study', a database that contains information on donors' choices among 64 nonprofits. Analysis of the database revealed that higher social status individuals tended to give to cultural organisations, whereas politically left-of-centre people were inclined to donate to nonprofits that had an international focus. Another interesting study in the area was a survey of 1,010 members of the general public in Austria conducted by Neumayr and Handy (2019) which asked people to state whether, within the previous 12 months, they had given to any or all of eight different types of cause. The study examined the sample members' personality traits, education, and income levels and assessed the possible effects of these variables on the type of cause to which a person had donated. It emerged that the participants' levels of 'generalised trust' (i.e., the general propensity to trust other people and organisations in most circumstances) were positively and significantly related to donating to international relief organisations and to religious institutions. However, generalised trust was negatively associated with the sample members' support for domestic social services. Empathetic concern was significantly linked to donating to domestic social services, to international relief, and to health nonprofits. Religiosity was a negative determinant of support for environmental protection organisations and social services.

Donors' trust in a charity has routinely been found to comprise a major determinant of willingness to give. Chapman, Hornsey, and Gillespie (2021) conducted a systematic literature review of 42 articles dealing with this matter published across 31 countries between 1988 and 2020. Outcomes confirmed the existence of positive associations between both organisational and sectoral trust on the one hand, and donation levels on the other. This was the case regardless of what other variables had been included in a study and irrespective of how trust was measured. The relationship was stronger in non-western countries, although most studies assessed donation intention rather than actual behaviour. A German study of 1,686 donors to 102 nonprofit organisations completed by Becker, Boenigk, and Willems (2020) identified four significant sociodemographic influences on trust in charities: age, gender, household size, and income. Older people and females were more trusting of charities, as were households containing more members and low-income individuals. However, neither religion nor education level exerted any significant effect. As regards, organisational considerations, accountability, the charity's mission, history, and size all influenced public trust in nonprofit organisations. Children's charities were significantly more trusted than others. Australian data examined by Wymer, Becker, and Boenigk (2020) revealed that, among 1,377 donors, organisational transparency exerted strong influences on trust, followed by an individual's awareness of the work of an organisation. In this study, gender was not found to have a significant effect.

Bennett (2012) observed that individuals who made regular donations to nonprofits usually gave to more than one organisation and, in over 75% of cases, the donations went to substantially different types of cause (e.g., giving to both a human service nonprofit and an animal protection charity). The author completed a survey the outcomes to which concluded that donors often obtained greater emotional benefit from supporting disparate genres of cause rather than just one cause. Variables found to affect the choice of the second nonprofit that a person supported were (i) the extent to which a second type of cause provided a good fit with a donor's self-image and (ii) the level of an individual's general desire for variation. Donors, it seemed, felt a need for 'cognitive balance' vis-à-vis the types of cause to which they gave money. These findings were compatible to those of an earlier study by Bennett and

Ali-Choudhury (2009) which examined the factors that encouraged people who, having made a charity donation for the first-time ever, would go on to make a second gift to the same organisation or to another charity. According to Bennett and Ali-Choudhury (2009), an initial decision to give to charity (regardless of the particular charity receiving the gift) induced a positive change in a first-time donor's 'mind-set' (i.e., a general attitude) towards charity giving. This change in mind-set caused a first-time donor to think more carefully and extensively about charities and their activities. When activated, the change in mind-set could increase the probability that the person would make a further donation, possibly to a charity in a field unrelated to that of the charity which triggered the change in mind-set in the first instance. The authors surveyed 551 recent first-time donors to charity who had subsequently made a second gift, finding that a change in mind-set regarding charity giving could impel a first-time donor to make a second gift. In 78% of cases, the second charity was in a different sector to that of the organisation receiving the initial gift. Other variables influencing decisions to make a second gift to (any) charity were the image and reputation of the organisation receiving the second gift, information overload with respect to the communications received from the first charity (this variable exerting a negative influence), the degree of warm glow experienced when giving to the second charity, and congruence between the values of the donor and the charity receiving the second gift. The factors that induced a person to make the second gift to a charity in a sector different to that of the first were the reputation and image of the second charity, and congruence of the second charity's values with those of the donor influences of the charity donation choices of friends, relatives, workmates, etc., and personal inertia (which had a negative effect).

A major concern in the study of the determinants of donors' choices of the types of good cause they are willing to support relates to factors that could induce people to support unpopular causes (e.g., homelessness, help for asylum seekers, prisoner rehabilitation), as opposed to highly popular causes such as child protection or cancer research. A paper by Body and Breeze (2016) explored this matter in detail and suggested that, in aggregate, lack of support for unpopular causes might be explained by 'Crowding Out Theory'. Thus, donations to highly popular causes might crowd out donations to others. The authors proposed that 'Labelling Theory' could also help explain the general absence of support for unpopular causes. Labelling Theory refers to the degree to which labels are perceived to reflect the innate characteristics of an entity. Thus, if a nonprofit labels itself as one that deals with an unpopular cause, the labelling *itself* will deter donors. Yet, another theory that could explain gifts to unpopular causes, the authors continued, was 'Sympathy Construction Theory', which posits that certain donors will subjectively construct sympathy for a particular cause based on their own personal experiences and the social worlds they inhabit. The last of these considerations, the social worlds in which individuals reside, raises the question of whether pressures exerted by third parties influence significantly people's choices of the nonprofits they are prepared to support? This issue was examined experimentally by Brown, Meer, and Williams (2017) who presented some, but not all, of their test subjects with third-party ratings of the quality of each of a number of nonprofits. The quality ratings employed were three or four-star ratings given by the 'Charity Navigator' organisation. All the participants were then asked to select the nonprofits to which they would donate. It emerged that the people who had been given the third-party ratings were more likely to choose nonprofits that were rated highly by the third party. This finding implied that the pursuit by fundraising nonprofits of high ratings in the publications of the main nonprofit ranking organisations was financially worthwhile, even though a proportion of nonprofit revenues would have to be devoted to the activities needed to obtain high rankings.

Nudging towards donation

A topic relating to individual giving that to date has received little attention but which deserves serious consideration is the application of 'Nudge Theory' to fundraising. A UK government sponsored report on this matter (Cabinet Office, 2013) offered a number of suggestions for 'nudging' people towards making charitable donations. It was important, the report stated, to make it easy for individuals to donate. Messages to donors from fundraisers should point out that by allowing a recipient nonprofit automatically to increase future payments, donors prevent a gift being eroded by inflation. 'Prompts' rather than conventional appeals should be used to encourage people to give, e.g., by setting a small charity donation from employees' monthly salaries as the default option (with an opt-out option) for new recruits. However, Hobbs (2017) challenged the usefulness of Nudge Theory as a fundraising mechanism on the grounds that, although nudges were a 'less complex and less normatively problematic' way of attempting to create positive attitudes (and hence donations) to a cause, they were inadequate because they aimed to bypass reflection about the cause. Circumventing reflection meant that donors who had been nudged into giving to a charity might then forget about the need for government action to remedy the underlying factors giving rise to the problem that the charity had been formed to address. Nudge Theory favoured motives over consequences, Hobbs (2017) alleged; nudging did little more than prompt an action (making a donation) but without changing the public's underlying attitudes and dispositions regarding a cause.

A defence of the use of nudging by fundraisers was presented by Ruehle, Engelen, and Archer (2021), who argued that several of the ethical objections raised against nudges (e.g., the exploitation of power they might involve and their arguably intrusive and deceptive nature) are not specific to nudging per se. Such problems could be avoided by carefully designed nudges. Indeed, the authors contended, infringements of donors' autonomy could be justified in certain circumstances. Ruehle et al. (2021) differentiated between 'perfect duties' undertaken by charities, imperfect duties, and 'supererogatory acts'. Examples of perfect duties were soliciting donations to disaster relief, for medical care, and for hunger prevention. Autonomy infringements were acceptable if a nudge fulfilled a perfect duty. Imperfect duties (e.g., promoting beneficiaries' happiness by donating to deprived children's education or donating to environmental conversation) could also be morally permissible. However, nudges that promoted supererogatory acts (for example, donations to arts organisations, the conservation of buildings, and funding for events that are not essential) were rarely permissible.

An interesting empirical study with results that fit with Nudge Theory was completed by Jacob, Gueguen, and Boulby (2018), who found that the 'visibility' of previous donations to a cause affects people's decisions to give to the same cause. Firstly, the authors placed collection boxes on the counters of ten French bakeries, the boxes being transparent on some days and opaque on others. More money was placed in the transparent boxes. Next, 180 store customers were approached by fundraisers who carried either a transparent

---

Box 2.3   Research opportunities: individual giving

Past research has demonstrated that decisions to give are complex and multifaceted. Thus, future research in the area might best proceed through interdisciplinary investigations of specific parts of broader models. Qualitative studies could yield richer and more meaningful results than quantitative research, as the statistical estimation of a sub-section of a larger model can lead to 'missing variable bias' and hence to unreliable values of estimated coefficients. (Models subjected to statistical analysis need to include independent variables that substantially explain the dependent variable(s) in a study; otherwise, technical problems create biases in the magnitudes of the parameters calculated in the course of an investigation.) Specific issues requiring research in the individual giving area include detailed explorations of (i) the influences of family members, friends, and associates on a person's attitude to charities and to particular causes; (ii) the effects of economic swings and austerity on people's perceptions of charity beneficiaries (e.g., whether perceptions become unfavourable during prosperous periods); and (iii) the consequences of changes over time in variables incorporated into models. Nudge Theory merits further research. Comparisons of the consequences of nudge-based appeals could be compared with the effects of traditional fundraising methods.

collection box or an opaque box. Again, more donations were placed in the transparent boxes. Finally, 240 residents of a French middle-income housing area were solicited at home for a clothing donation. Approaches were made either holding a transparent bag containing several items of clothing or with no items. More people gave clothing when the saw several garments in a bag. Jacob et al. (2018) used Social Proof Theory to explain their results. Social Proof Theory relates to the phenomenon whereby individuals observe the behaviour of those around them in order to make a decision.

Effects of income and social status

An aspect of individual giving that has attracted a considerable amount of attention among nonprofit researchers on both sides of the Atlantic concerns the observed disparity between the percentages of people's incomes donated to nonprofits by the rich and the poor sections of society. Research (and government data) has firmly established that, on the average, financially poor people donate proportionately more of their incomes to nonprofits than better-off individuals. A large amount of evidence supports this proposition. For example, analysis of the 105,731 replies to the UK government's annual Citizenship Survey for the years between 2001 and 2011 shows that the poorest 20% of the UK population gave an average of 3.2% of their incomes to charity, compared with 0.9% for the richest 20% (the remaining 60% donated an average of 2%). In the USA, average donation percentages of 3.2% for the poor and 1.3% for the financially well-off are normal. From a variety of sources, it seems that the average percentage of income donated by the poor lies somewhere between 3% and 3.5%, and by the well-off is about 1% (for information on these matters, see Wiepking, 2007; Bennett, 2011). Studies have shown moreover that observed differences cannot be attributed to over-representations of young or elderly people in samples. Arguably, younger individuals might expect their incomes to rise in the future and hence may give generously now, even though they are currently poor, while older people have been found to be generally more generous than the middle-aged. However, the annual '*UK Giving*' surveys conducted by the Charities Aid Foundation have concluded that low-income old and low-income young individuals tend to give proportionately more of their incomes to charity than do wealthier old and young donors.

Reasons advanced for this situation include possibilities that the financially well-off are more likely than the poor to prioritise their own self-interests above the well-being of others; that the rich have a greater tendency to want to accumulate wealth; that the wealthy experience first-hand the problems dealt with by nonprofits less frequently; and/or that the rich have less empathy with the suffering of poorer people who are in need. The latter proposition is reinforced by survey findings that wealthy individuals tend not to support nonprofits that serve the poor and the dispossessed, and vice versa for poorer people. Piff, Kraus, Cote, Cheng, and Keltner (2010) reported an 'emerging body of literature' which has concluded that personal engagement with the 'needs of others', as opposed to 'focusing on one's own welfare', best explains giving behaviour among low social class individuals (p. 771). The poor give relatively more, Piff et al. (2010) argued, 'because of greater commitment to egalitarian values and feelings of compassion' (p. 771).

This line of reasoning was pursued by Bennett (2011) in a study of the nonprofit giving behaviour of low-income donors in deprived areas in London. The author found that 'standard' variables (altruism, empathy, etc.) affected donation levels and frequency, as did an individual's sense of affinity with other low-income people and the person's beliefs regarding the degree to which the poor are treated unfairly by society. Wiepking (2007) offered a somewhat different explanation for why the average percentage of income donated by the wealthy is relatively low. The author analysed 1587 responses to the 'Giving in the Netherlands Panel Study', concluding that a certain 'giving standard' existed among the panel participants and that this giving standard could explain why the wealthy people in the sample gave proportionately less. Both the rich and the poor, Wiepking (2007) argued, have in their minds a 'giving standard' regarding how much money they should donate. The giving standard exists in people's minds in *absolute*, not relative, terms, and critically, the giving standard of financially well-off people is not much higher than the giving standard of the poor. Therefore, Wiepking (2007) concluded, the percentage of income donated by wealthy individuals will normally be less than that of people whose incomes are low.

Box 2.4   Research opportunities: why the poor give more

Future research into the differences between the giving behaviour of the rich and the poor could usefully examine disparities in attitudes towards personal saving within each group (e.g., whether high levels of personal saving are inversely related to charity giving); differences in levels of trust in nonprofit organisations and whether intention–behaviour links are the same among richer and poorer people. Compared to financially better-off individuals, poorer people are known to 'overspend'. Could this tendency help to explain relatively generous charity giving? Also, to the extent that rich people engage in 'luxury consumption', do they expect 'luxury services' from the charities they support? If the latter is the case, charities need to treat rich donors in ways that are quite different to those applied to financially poor supporters.

Giving by businesses

In the UK, the FTSE 100 companies annually give an average of nearly 2% of their pre-tax incomes to charity (although the ten biggest donors account for about 70% of the total value of all FTSE 100 donations). Enterprises may give to a nonprofit organisation without any expectation of commercial reward, might engage in CRM, may sponsor nonprofits, or can participate in other types of collaborative arrangements between businesses and nonprofits. These other forms of association are increasingly sophisticated and extend to licensing agreements, joint issue promotions, strategic alliances, and joint ventures. (Wymer and Samu [2003] provide a comprehensive typology of the various categories of relationships between businesses and nonprofits.)

Since corporate giving to good causes can be driven mainly by purely philanthropic motives, by commercial self-interest, or by both, the balance between altruistic and business reasons for donating to nonprofits ('doing good versus doing well') has been keenly debated in academic circles. Ethical issues associated with the philanthropic activities of businesses were examined in a seminal work by Burlingame and Young (1996), who identified four 'ethical models' of corporate philanthropy practices. Model one was the 'neoclassical/corporate productivity model' which is based on enlightened self-interest and the view that corporate philanthropy should contribute to a company's long-run profits. Model two was the 'ethical/altruistic model' which posits that a business should use part of its revenues to do what is right for society because society itself nurtures the success of the enterprise. The third model was the 'political model' which suggests that corporates sometimes seek to build relationships with nonprofits and to embed themselves in society in order to avoid government regulation. Model four was the 'stakeholder model' which is based on the proposition that a main purpose of corporate philanthropy is to appease stakeholders, hopefully to make them pleased with a company's management.

Another interesting paper relating to the ethical propriety of corporate philanthropy was authored by Godfrey (2005) who discussed the 'moral' dimensions of the practice. Corporate philanthropy, Godfrey (2005) argued, generates positive moral capital both among stakeholders and within the communities in which a business operates. Moral capital (defined as the moral values imputed to an organisation's philanthropic activities) then provides the enterprise with 'insurance' that will protect its reputational assets in future dealings with stakeholders and communities. This protection increased shareholder wealth, Godfrey (2005) concluded. Hence, corporate philanthropy offered benefits to all parties: the nonprofit and its stakeholders, the community, and the businesses that make donations.

Research into the topic of corporate philanthropy has been extensive although, according to a comprehensive and insightful analysis by Likert and Simaens (2015), studies have been fragmented and scattered across many different fields. This diffusion of corporate philanthropy research, Likert and Simaens (2015) continued, has 'resulted in a rather loose field of theorising' on the subject (p. 285). The authors reviewed 122 articles on corporate philanthropy, concluding that there was no consensus in the literature on the determinants of corporate philanthropy, or even on the conceptualisation of the subject. Instead, conceptualisations were based on many different theoretical bases that ranged through Institutional Theory, Stakeholder Theory, theories of justice, psychological needs theories, and several other approaches. The authors concluded that a major gap in the research literature existed regarding knowledge about the effects of corporate philanthropy on society, as opposed to its impacts on companies or on the causes that businesses support. It was important, moreover, that corporate philanthropy research be clearly differentiated from the broader notion of corporate social responsibility (i.e., actions that foster social good beyond an enterprise's interests and over and above what is required by law). A sharp distinction between corporate philanthropy and corporate social responsibility was necessary in order to 'improve conceptual precision' and to assist in the measurement of constructs in the cause of research (p. 301). Future investigations of corporate philanthropy should, the authors suggested, concentrate on deep qualitative case studies rather than quantitative research. This was because a large amount of past research in the field had been based on data collected mainly because of its ease of access, e.g., from companies' own annual reports and from company websites, and such data did not necessarily reveal much about the decision processes underlying gifts.

The extent of the proliferation of research into corporate philanthropy was described in papers by Gautier and Pache (2015) and by Cha and Rajadhyaksha (2021). Gautier and Pache (2015) reviewed 162 papers on the subject published in the 30 years prior to 2015. The authors identified four genres of articles dealing with the subject, namely, (i) definitions of 'what corporate philanthropy is' (noting that no consensus exists on the definition of corporate philanthropy), (ii) presumptions regarding the drivers of corporate philanthropy, (iii) descriptions of how corporate philanthropy is organised within and by companies, and (iv) reports of the performance outcomes to the employment of corporate philanthropy. Often, Gautier and Pache (2015) continued that research involved consumer surveys and experiments that varied particular consumer behaviour variables within models (usually structural equation models) that sought to explain purchase intention. Different mediators and moderators had been included in model configurations, disparate message types and advertisement framing techniques had been examined, different price manipulations had been used in experiments, and so on. Cha and Rajadhyaksha (2021) critically reviewed 60 years of research covering 228 corporate philanthropy documents (including 214 journal articles, 5 dissertations, and 9 books and book chapters) across and between disciplines. The authors devised a multi-level and multidisciplinary theoretical framework that synthesises and integrated the corporate philanthropy literature at micro-, meso-, and macro-levels of analysis.

Major criticisms of corporate philanthropy are that (i) it can cause mission drift (see Chapter 1) because recipient nonprofits may become accountable more to their corporate donors than to other stakeholders, (ii) 'free riders' may benefit from favourable publicity surrounding a large gift by a business operating in a particular industry cluster that contains the donating company's competitors, and (iii) shareholders in a donating enterprise are wrongfully deprived of funds. Another accusation is that, in some cases, corporate philanthropy represents little more than 'conscience laundering' by companies that in their normal operations engage in unethical activities (e.g., polluting the physical environment or exploiting third world workers). The allegation that corporate philanthropy dispossesses shareholders of what is rightfully theirs was investigated by Masulis and Reza (2014), who examined the financial records and company reports for the period 1996–2006 of 406 of the USA's Fortune 500 companies together with data extracted from the US National Directory of Corporate Giving. Masulis and Reza (2014) found that 71% of the gifts made by the sample companies went to charities with which the company's chief executive officer (CEO) had a personal connection. There was, moreover, a 69% overlap between the charitable causes supported by the sample enterprises and the charitable interests of the companies' independent directors. Increases in expenditures on corporate philanthropy were positively and significantly associated with rises in CEO compensation. This finding might be due, the authors suggested, to CEOs directing their companies' charitable donations towards the nonprofits in which independent directors had interests. Masulis and Reza (2014) argued that the values of shareholders' cash holdings were (substantially) reduced by this situation. Corporate philanthropy advanced CEOs' welfare, but not that of shareholders. Hence, the authors concluded, regulators should compel companies to disclose publicly the details of all insider-affiliated corporate giving. This line of enquiry could usefully be followed up by studies of the influences of the personal interests of middle managers who help take decisions about the directions of an enterprise's philanthropic activities.

Arguably, conspicuous reporting of corporate philanthropy can enhance a company's reputation. Potential connections between corporate philanthropy and an enterprise's reputation were investigated by Gardberg, Zyglidopoulos, Symeou, and Schepers (2017) via an analysis of data collected by the Reputation Institute on the evaluations of the reputations of 60 large companies by 33,562 individuals. The authors employed Signal Detection Theory to measure the effects on a company's 'reputation for corporate social performance' of a company's 'signal amplitude' (measured as the amounts it had given to good causes); of 'signal dispersion' (the number of causes supported); and of 'signal consistency' (i.e., whether or not the company had set up a foundation to manage its donation activities). People's assessments of an enterprise's corporate social performance were measured by (i) their responses to the social responsibility items in the Reputation Institute's 'Reputation Quotient' scale (this variable being termed as corporate social responsibility 'perceptions') and (ii) their answers to a question concerning their level of knowledge of a company's social responsibility activities (termed as corporate social responsibility 'awareness'). Findings indicated that all three elements of a company's signals influenced awareness of its social responsibility activities, as did the nature of a company's portfolio of corporate philanthropy activities. Awareness itself helped determine corporate social responsibility perceptions.

An important question is whether corporate philanthropy improves a company's overall performance, e.g., via better employee motivation consequent to employees knowing that a business is giving to charity, or through consumers deciding to buy more of the enterprise's products. Godfrey (2005) noted that over 100 studies on corporate philanthropy had been published prior to 2005 and that outcomes concerning whether the practice *actually* improved corporate financial performance had been mixed. Many problems had diminished the reliability of empirical results obtained from these studies, Godfrey (2005) concluded, including errors in statistical methodology, inadequate data, dubious sources of information, and issues to do with choices of independent and dependent variables. Notwithstanding these difficulties, Seifert, Morris, and Bartkus (2004) completed a valuable analysis of the cash flow records of the Fortune 1,000 companies, finding a strong positive correlation between companies' favourable cash flow positions and the amounts they gave to good causes. However, there was no significant connection between corporate giving and overall financial performance.

Another crucial issue in the corporate philanthropy field is whether adverse market conditions reduce or stimulate corporate giving. The latter situation might arise if businesses perceive corporate giving to constitute a source of competitive advantage that needs to be increased during economic downturns (analogous to companies increasing their advertising expenditures whenever revenues begin to fall). Catalao-Lopez, Pina, and Branca (2016) investigated this matter by completing econometric tests on US data over the period from 1990 to 2012 to ascertain the effects of the business cycle on corporate philanthropy. Results indicated that US businesses did reduce their donations during downturns, but only in the short term, donations returned to previous levels within a few years following a downturn.

Box 2.5   Research opportunities: corporate philanthropy

Further research on corporate philanthropy could focus on its effects on the *beneficiaries* of recipient nonprofits; given that prior studies have arguably been 'giver-centric' in approach and have concentrated on the impact of corporate philanthropy on nonprofit organisations rather than on the people, the nonprofits were established to help. These effects on beneficiaries need to be measured in a rigorous fashion, possibly in the context of comprehensive and integrated predictive models that contain relevant mediating and moderating variables. Industry sector studies and comparisons would be useful, as would the development of scales to measure specific elements of companies' corporate philanthropy activities. Research should aim perhaps at revealing 'best practices' relating to company giving, having regard for the need to establish rigorous and meaningful criteria for defining 'best practices'. Another interesting area for future research relates to whether the corporate philanthropy function has been 'professionalised' in companies and in nonprofits, and if it has, what are the antecedents and consequences of professionalisation?

Cause-related marketing

CRM relates to the situation that arises when a business promotes or assists a nonprofit's cause by publicising that a proportion of its profits or sales will be devoted to the nonprofit's cause. CRM seeks *overtly* to link the buying public's positive attitudes towards a nonprofit organisation to the image of the sponsoring company or brand. The emphasis is as much on what a charity can do for the business as on the financial benefits to the charity. Opinions differ as to whether corporate involvement in CRM is driven fundamentally by the profit motive rather than by altruism. If CRM is motivated by the pursuit of commercial advantage, the practice needs to be regarded as a hard-headed business investment. Otherwise, the application of commercial principles to the management of CRM might not be appropriate. Advocates of the proposition that CRM should be seen as a commercial rather than philanthropic activity argue that (i) corporate support for a good cause is essentially a product that should be professionally marketed, (ii) by increasing business revenues a firm generates the profits necessary to fund additional donations, and (iii) the company's own customers and employees may themselves be encouraged to give to a particular cause consequent to the publicity surrounding a company's involvement with the cause.

Academic research into these matters was stimulated by a highly influential paper authored by Varadarajan and Menon (1988) which, having surveyed the CRM landscape and having reviewed past literature on CRM, then defined the basic elements and constructs associated with CRM, outlined the various forms that CRM might assume, and examined the benefits and drawbacks of CRM from both corporate and societal points of view. Varadarajan and Menon (1988) listed numerous questions for future CRM research, thus triggering a multitude of investigations. Hundreds of articles have been published on CRM, and few aspects of the topic remain unexplored. However, a difficulty with much of the research on the subject, according to Godfrey (2005), has been the absence of theoretical foundations within studies. Lafferty, Lueth, and McCafferty (2016) sought to provide a theoretical foundation for CRM research. The authors recognised that CRM 'has become almost ubiquitous as brands of all price points participate in this marketing strategy, in the United States and internationally' (p. 951) and thus proposed an 'Evolutionary Process Model' to explain how CRM strategies had evolved over time, had been applied in the past, and were used currently. The model was developed within a conceptual paper and involved factors concerning the goodness-of-fit between a charitable cause and the company's brand(s), corporate strategies, consumers' financial and social responses, and consumer feedback mechanisms. A systematic review of the (then) past literature on the subject enabled Lafferty et al. (2016) to suggest lists of independent and dependent variables that could be used to measure each of these considerations.

Another systematic literature review of CRM research completed by Thomas, Kureshi, and Vatavwala (2020) covered 202 articles published in peer-reviewed academic journals over a period of 28 years. The authors concluded that attribution theory was the most popular theory applied to the analysis of the phenomenon, with a majority of the articles focusing on business-planning aspects of the subject. Attributions ascribed to cause-related products typically depended on customers' perceptions regarding the product's industry, brand, and the supplying company. Other common theories used to analyse CRM practices involved persuasion theory (see below), associative learning theory, the theory of reasoned action, and self-construal theory. (Associative learning theory explores the creation of associative networks between an organisation and a supported charity or cause, emphasising the need for a good fit between the cause and a business.)

Consumer attitudes towards CRM

Many studies have explored specific variables capable of affecting consumer attitudes towards CRM. Examples include the investigations of Ladero, Casquet, and Singh (2014), who examined a person's 'susceptibility to interpersonal influence' and personal values as determinants of attitudes regarding CRM; and Patel, Gadhavi, and Shukla's (2017) who scrutinised the role of 'personal scepticism' in forming attitudes and purchase intention. Ladero et al.'s (2014) study surveyed 456 consumers, concluding that (i) sociodemographic characteristics affected personal values, which in turn impacted on attitudes concerning CRM, (ii) susceptibility to interpersonal influence influenced how heavily personal values figured in attitude formation, and (iii) values helped determine attitudes to CRM. Patel et al. (2017) found, via a survey of 424 consumers in western India, that scepticism regarding the true intentions of companies engaging in CRM had no discernible negative effect on either attitude towards a company marketing or intentions to purchase the company's products. CRM did improve attitude to the brand and to purchase intention, the authors concluded. Amawate and Deb (2021) claimed that there has been an increase in the number of sceptical consumers who do not trust the actions of marketers and that this extended to CRM. Their survey of 500 consumers across five cities suggested that higher awareness of CRM could lead to higher scepticism. Younger consumers and females were found to be less sceptical about CRM.

A substantial amount of evidence suggests that consumers generally support CRM (see the paper by Polonsky and MacDonald, 2000) and that they are willing to switch brands to a cause-related alternative provided the price of the latter is not excessively high. Nevertheless, negative opinions of CRM might arise among people who suspect that businesses and nonprofits are attempting to influence their attitudes and behaviour. This possibility was investigated by Hamby and Brinberg (2017), who developed a scale to measure consumers' CRM persuasion knowledge, i.e., the extents to which consumers recognised the presence of CRM when buying goods and how they evaluated the various elements of CRM campaigns. The authors observed that 'current CRM practices are likely to exacerbate consumer confusion because there is no standard format to present information about the link between a purchase and the corporate transfer of resources (e.g., money) to the NP organization' (p. 5). Thus, a measure of the presence of such confusion among consumers was required. Persuasion knowledge was defined as a consumer's beliefs about the motives underlying a promotional effort, about who benefits (the consumer or the business), and about whether the tactics employed in the promotion are appropriate. A 23-item scale was created with dimensions relating to a consumer's knowledge of benefits to the company, the goodness-of-fit of the company to the nonprofit, and the level of a consumer's knowledge that a purchase was necessary before the nonprofit received any benefit from the business. The persuasive dimension of CRM was examined in depth in study by Bergkvist and Zhou (2019) who, on the basis of a review of the literature on CRM persuasion research (i.e., studies of how CRM influences evaluations of the partner brand), developed a model of Leveraged Marketing Communications (LMC), according to which CRM affects brand evaluations along two paths: an indirect transfer path mediated by attribution of motives and the direct transfer path in which attitude towards the cause is transferred to the brand.

Most (though not all) of the numerous surveys of attitudes and behaviour concerning CRM have found that men and women respond differently to CRM. These studies have typically concluded that women are somewhat more favourably inclined towards the practice. An interesting study relevant to this issue was completed by Williams (2003) who examined the relationship between the proportion of women serving on corporate boards of directors in Fortune 150 companies between 1991 and 1994 and the extents of charitable giving by these companies during the period. The connection was positive and highly significant. Also, the companies with higher proportions of women on their boards were more likely than others to donate to arts and community service nonprofits. A related study involving the role of women on boards in connection with corporate giving was that of Cha and Abebe (2016), who employed 'Stakeholder Theory' (i.e., 'the theory that the extent to which a business builds a relationship with certain stakeholders is closely tied to the personal and social backgrounds of board members' [p. 672]) in order to explore possible relationships between the numbers of females on company boards and companies' levels of corporate philanthropy. Multi-year data on the donations of 104 US corporations were inspected and revealed a positive and significant relationship. The data also showed that (i) there was no discernible link between the number of external (non-executive) board members and the amounts that companies gave to charities, and (ii) corporate philanthropy was often used to protect businesses' reputations consequent to reputational challenges (product recalls or dysfunctions for example).

Box 2.6   Research opportunities: cause-related marketing

A multitude of studies have been undertaken into CRM, so future research in the field needs to be carefully targeted, parsimonious, and not simply to repeat investigations of issues that have already been covered. Remaining CRM-related research questions include the criteria to be employed when dividing the profits arising from a successful campaign (including the issue of whether the nonprofit partner should benefit from the appreciation of a company's share price [a subject suggested as far back as 2003 by Wymer and Samu (2003) but still under-researched]), and how decisions are formulated regarding whether a potential partner is a 'good fit' with the other organisation. As regards, the latter issue, i.e., the goodness-of-fit between the parties, to what extent are the views of a nonprofit's *beneficiaries* taken into account when a partner is being selected? Other matters worthy of detailed investigation concern the sources of power of each partner and how these sources impact on marketing decisions, and the roles of trust and commitment in the nonprofit–business collaboration context. Two additional topics that deserve future research are (i) whether customers who purchase CRM products actually (as is sometimes alleged) reduce the amounts they otherwise give to charity and, if so, why, and (ii) whether companies' CRM programmes change as levels of competitive intensity within the sectors in which they operate alter?

Sponsorship

Corporate sponsorship is a common means through which businesses support charitable organisations. It involves the purchase by a business (in cash or kind) of an association with a charitable event or activity in return for the commercial potential linked to the event or activity. Allegedly, the sponsorship of a nonprofit organisation can improve consumers' perceptions of the sponsoring business through linking consumers' beliefs about the business to an enjoyable charitable event or activity and might influence the perceptions of the enterprise that is held by shareholders, employees, financiers, the media, pressure groups, and local and national government. Businesses that engage in sponsorship may or may not expect a financial return from a sponsored activity.

Sponsorship of nonprofits has been most common perhaps in relation to sports events and art exhibitions. Filo, Funk, and O'Brien (2010) used the Psychological Continuum Model to examine the effects of taking part in a charity sports event on participants' attitudes towards the sponsor. (The Psychological Continuum Model is a framework that seeks to explain sports participation behaviour in terms of a progressive development from awareness to attraction, attachment, and allegiance.) The model was tested on a sample of 672 individuals, all of whom had paid an entry fee to the charity for participation in an event. The results suggested that the participants' recreational and philanthropic motives contributed to 'attachment to the event', while event attachment and charitable motives contributed to the participants' favourable perceptions of the corporate sponsor's image. These outcomes implied a greater willingness of participants to purchase the sponsoring company's products. It is relevant to note that sponsors can help nonprofits in various ways other than by donating money, e.g., via the transfer of business know-how, provision of training, or staff secondments. This matter was investigated by Alvarez-Gonzales, Garcia-Rodriguez, Rey-Garcia, and Sanza-Perez (2017), who found positive and significant relationships between successful business–nonprofit partnerships and improvements in the internal capabilities of the nonprofits studied. Enhancement of internal capabilities included greater levels of professionalism and higher degrees of market orientation (see Chapter 1), which in turn led to superior fundraising performance. Fechner, Filo, Reid, and Cameron (2022) reviewed 42 English journal articles, focusing on the managerial implications advanced within the corporate sports sponsorship literature. The authors concluded that careful segmentation of people attending an event was necessary in order to create meaningful sponsorship initiatives. Also, event sponsors should share their underlying motivation to support their sponsorships and should invite employees to volunteer at events. Sometimes, a sponsor will conspicuously 'match' any amounts given to a particular nonprofit by members of the public. Meer (2017) investigated this situation, finding that the practice of sponsoring companies matching the donations made by individual consumers did tend to increase the public's willingness to give to a sponsored nonprofit. Moreover, if competing businesses decided to match public donations to other nonprofits, this did not reduce levels of giving to the first nonprofit.

A related form of corporate support relates to the practice of supermarkets and other stores providing, at checkout points, opportunities for shoppers to donate to a cause favoured by a business. Obeng, Nakhata, and Kuo (2019) noted the paucity of research into the factors that induce customers to give in this way. The authors contributed to knowledge in the area by studying the relationship between superior retail service and shoppers' willingness to donate at a checkout. They concluded that customers who believed they had experienced superior service were grateful to the retailer and thus reciprocated their gratitude by being more willing to donate. Some retailers seek to increase checkout donations by pairing donation requests with default options. Crow, Mathmann, and Greer (2019) conducted an experiment involving 216 US non-student adults in order to investigate whether people who felt a deep 'need for locomotion' (i.e., the need to exercise control while making decisions) were more or less likely to accept a high or low default option. Low locomotion was found to increase donations in the presence of defaults. A similar experiment was undertaken by Sudbury and Vossler (2022) who presented 896 students with three popular point-of-sale solicitation mechanisms: a rounding request (i.e., yes or no to an amount based on a store transaction); a fixed donation request (i.e., a request to donate an amount unrelated to the transaction); and an open-ended request for a gift. Donation rates were highest for the rounding mechanism. Differences in donation amounts between the rounding and fixed request options seemed to depend on 'loose change effects', i.e., people were more likely to donate when doing so reduced the amount of change they received from a transaction.

References

Alvarez-Gonzales, L., Garcia-Rodriguez, N., Rey-Garcia, M. and Sanza-Perez. (2017) "Business-Nonprofit Partnerships as a Driver of Internal Marketing in Nonprofit Organisations: Consequences for Nonprofit Moderators", *Business Research Quarterly* 20 (2), 112–123.

Amawate, V. and Deb, M. (2021) "Antecedents and Consequences of Consumer Skepticism Toward Cause-Related Marketing: Gender as Moderator and Attitude as Mediator", *Journal of Marketing Communications* 27 (1), 31–52.

Andreoni, J. (1990) "Impure Altruism and Donations to Public Goods: A Theory of Warm Glow Giving", *Economic Journal* 100, 464–477.

Becker, A., Boenigk, S. and Willems, J. (2020) "In Nonprofits We Trust? A Large-Scale Study on the Public's Trust in Nonprofit Organizations", *Journal of Nonprofit and Public Sector Marketing* 32 (2), 189–216.

Bekkers, R. and Wiepking, P. (2011) "A Literature Review of Empirical Studies on Philanthropy: Eight Mechanisms that Drive Charity Giving", *Nonprofit and Voluntary Sector Quarterly* 40 (5), 924–973.

Bendapudi, N., Singh, S. and Bendapudi, V. (1996) "Enhancing Helping Behaviour: An Integrative Framework for Promotion Planning", *Journal of Marketing* 60 (3), 33–54.

Bennett, R. (2003) "Factors Underlying the Inclination to Donate to Particular Types of Charity", *International Journal of Nonprofit and Voluntary Sector Marketing* 8 (1), 12–29.

Bennett, R. (2011) "Why Urban Poor Donate: A Study of Low-income Charitable Giving in London", *Nonprofit and Voluntary Sector Quarterly* 41 (5), 870–891.

Bennett. R. (2012) "What Else Shall I Support? An Empirical Study of Multiple Cause Donation Behaviour", *Journal of Nonprofit and Voluntary Sector Marketing* 24 (1), 1–25.

Bennett, R. and Ali-Choudhury, R. (2009) "Second Gift Behaviour of First-Time Donors to Charity: An Empirical Study", *International Journal of Nonprofit and Voluntary Sector Marketing* 14 (3), 161–180.

Bergkvist, L. and Zhou, K. (2019) "Cause-Related Marketing Persuasion Research: An Integrated Framework and Directions for Further Research", *International Journal of Advertising* 38 (1), 5–25.

Bischoff, I. and Krauskopf, T. (2015) "Warm Glow of Giving Collectively: An Experimental Study", *Journal of Economic Psychology* 51, 210–218.

Block, S. (2000) "A History of the Discipline". In Ott, J. (Ed), *The Nature of the Nonprofit Sector: An Overview*, 97–111, Boulder CO: Westview Press.

Body, A. and Breeze, B. (2016) "What are 'Unpopular' Causes and How Do They Achieve Fundraising?", *International Journal of Nonprofit and Voluntary Sector Marketing* 21 (1), 57–70.

Brown, A., Meer, J. and Williams, J. (2017) "Social Distance and Quality Ratings in Charity Choice", *Journal of Behavioural and Experimental Economics* 66, 9–15.

Burgoyne, C., Young, B. and Walker, C. (2005) "Deciding to Give to Charity: A Focus Group Study in the Context of Household Economy", *Journal of Community and Applied Social Studies* 15 (5), 383–405.

Burlingame, D. and Young, D. (1996) *Corporate Philanthropy at the Crossroads*, Indiana: Indiana University Press.

Cabinet Office. (2013) *Applying Behavioural Insights to Charity Giving*, London: Cabinet Office and Charities Aid Foundation.

Carpenter, J. (2021) "The Shape of Warm Glow: Field Experimental Evidence from a Fundraiser", *Journal of Economic Behaviour and Organization* 191, 555–574.

Cataleo-Lopez, M., Pina, J. and Branca, A. (2016) "Social Responsibility, Corporate Giving and the Tide", *Management Decision* 54 (9), 2294–2309.

Cha, W. and Abebe, M. (2016) "Board of Directors and Industry Determinants of Corporate Philanthropy", *Leadership and Organisational Development Journal* 37 (5), 672–688.

Cha, W. and Rajadhyaksha, U. (2021) "What Do We Know About Corporate Philanthropy? A Review and Research Directions", *Business Ethics, the Environment and Responsibility* 30 (2), 262–286.

Chapman, C., Hornsey, M. and Gillespie, N. (2021) "To What Extent Is Trust a Prerequisite for Charitable Giving? A Systematic Review and Meta-Analysis", *Nonprofit and Voluntary Sector Quarterly* 50 (6), 1274–1303.

Cropanzano, R. and Mitchell, M. (2005) "Social Exchange Theory: An Interdisciplinary Review", *Journal of Management* 31 (6), 874–900.

Crow, K., Mathmann, F. and Greer, D. (2019) "Got a Dollar? Locomotion Orientation Decreases the Effect of Defaults on Charitable Giving", *Journal of Retailing and Consumer Services* 48, 1–6.

Denis, E., Pecheux, C. and Decrop, A. (2018) "Segmenting the Belgian Charity Sector: The Impact of Environmental Factors on Households' Generosity", *International Journal of Nonprofit and Voluntary Sector Marketing*, 23, e1606.

de Oliveira, A., Croson, R. and Eckel, C. (2011) "The Giving Type: Identifying Donors", *Journal of Public Economics* 95 (5/6), 428–435.

Fechner, D., Filo, K., Reid, S. and Cameron, R. (2022) "A Systematic Literature Review of Charity Sport Event Sponsorship", *European Sport Management Quarterly*, Early view, 1–23.

Filo, K., Funk, D. and O'Brien, D. (2010) "The Antecedents and Outcomes of Attachment and Sponsor Image Within Charity Sport Events", *Journal of Sport Management* 24, 623–648.

Gardberg, N., Zyglidopoulos, S., Symeou, P. and Schepers, D. (2017) "The Impact of Corporate Philanthropy on Reputation for Corporate Social Performance", *Business and Society* 58 (6) 1177–1208.

Gautier, A. and Pache, A. (2015) "Research on Corporate Philanthropy: A Review and Assessment", *Journal of Business Ethics* 126 (3), 343–369.

Godfrey, P. (2005) "The Relationship Between Corporate Philanthropy and Shareholder Wealth: A Risk Management Perspective", *Academy of Management Review* 30 (4), 777–798.

Hamby, A. and Brinberg, D. (2017) "Cause-Related Marketing Persuasion Knowledge: Measuring Consumers' Knowledge and Ability to Interpret Cause-Related Marketing Promotions", *Journal of Consumer Affairs* 52 (2), 373–392.

Hobbs, J. (2017) "Nudging Charitable Giving: The Ethics of Nudge in International Poverty Reduction", *Ethics and Global Politics* 10 (1), 37–57.

Homans, G. (1958) "Social Behaviour as Exchange", *American Journal of Sociology* 63 (5), 597–606.

Homans, G. (1974). *Social Behavior: Its Elementary Forms* (Revised ed.), London: Harcourt Brace Jovanovich.

Jacob, C., Gueguen, N. and Boulby, G. (2018) "How Proof of Previous Donations Influences Compliance with a Donation Request: Three Field Experiments", *International Review on Public and Nonprofit Marketing* 15 (1), 1–8.

Karlan, D. and Wood, D. (2017) "The Effect of Effectiveness in a Direct Mail Fundraising Experiment", *Journal of Behavioural and Experimental Economics* 66, 1–8.

Konrath, S. and Handy, F. (2018) "The Development and Validation of the Motives to Donate Scale", *Nonprofit and Voluntary Sector Quarterly* 47 (2), 347–375.

Kumar, A. and Chakrabarti, S. (2023) "Charity Donor Behaviour: A Systematic Literature Review and Research Agenda", *Journal of Nonprofit and Public Sector Marketing* 35 (1), 1–46.

Ladero, M., Casquet, C. and Singh, J. (2014) "Understanding Factors Influencing Consumer Attitudes to Cause-related Marketing", *International Journal of Nonprofit and Voluntary Sector Marketing* 20 (1), 52–70.

Lafferty, B., Lueth, A. and McCafferty, R. (2016) "An Evolutionary Process Model of Cause-Related Marketing and Systematic Review of the Empirical Literature", *Psychology and Marketing* 33 (11), 951–970.

Likert, K. and Simaens, A. (2015) "Battling the Devolution in the Research on Corporate Philanthropy", *Journal of Business Ethics* 126 (2), 285–308.

Mainardes, E., Laurett, R., Degasperi, N. and Lasso, S. (2016) "External Motivators for Donation of Money and/or Goods", *International Journal of Nonprofit and Voluntary Sector Marketing* 22 (2), e1568.

Masulis, R. and Reza, S. (2014) "Agency Problems of Corporate Philanthropy", *Review of Financial Studies* 28 (2), 592–636.

Mayo, J. and Tinsley, C. (2009) "Warm Glow and Charitable Giving: Why the Wealthy Do Not Give More to Charity?", *Journal of Economic Psychology* 30 (3), 490–499.

Meer, J. (2017) "Does Fundraising Create New Giving?", *Journal of Public Economics* 145, 82–93.

Neumayr, M. and Handy, F. (2019) "Charitable Giving: What Influences Donors' Choices Among Different Causes", *Voluntas* 30 (4), 783–799.

Obeng, E., Nakhata, C. and Kuo, H. (2019) "Paying it Forward: The Reciprocal Effect of Superior Service on Charity at Checkout", *Journal of Business Research* 98, 250–260.

Patel, J., Gadhavi, D. and Shukla, Y. (2017) "Consumers' Responses to Cause-related Marketing: Moderating Influences of Cause Involvement and Scepticism on Attitude and Purchase Intention", *International Review on Public and Nonprofit Marketing* 14 (1), 1–18.

Piff, P., Kraus, W., Cote, S., Cheng, B. and Keltner, D. (2010) "Having Less, Giving More: The Influence of Social Class on Prosocial Behaviour", *Journal of Personality and Social Psychology* 99 (5), 771–784.

Polonsky, M. and MacDonald, E. (2000) "Exploring the Link Between Cause-Related Marketing and Brand Building", *International Journal of Nonprofit and Voluntary Sector Marketing* 5 (1), 46–57.

Ruehle, R., Engelen, B. and Archer, A. (2021) "Nudging Charitable Giving: What (If Anything) Is Wrong with It?", *Nonprofit and Voluntary Sector Quarterly* 50 (2), 353–371.

Sargeant, A. (1999) "Charitable Giving: Toward a Model of Donor Behaviour", *Journal of Marketing Management* 15 (4), 215–238.

Sargeant, A. and Woodliffe, L. (2007) "Gift Giving: An Interdisciplinary Review", *International Journal of Nonprofit and Voluntary Sector Marketing* 12 (4), 275–307.

Schindler, S., Reinhard, M., Stahlberg, D. and Len, A. (2014) "Quid Pro Quo: The Effect of Individual's Exchange Orientation on Prosocial Behaviour and the Moderating Role of Mortality Salience", *Social Influence* 9 (4), 242–252.

Seifert, B., Morris, S. and Bartkus, B. (2004) "Having, Giving and Getting: Slack Resources, Corporate Philanthropy, and Firm Financial Performance", *Business and Society* 43 (2), 135–161.

Sneddon, J., Evers, U. and Lee, J (2020) "Personal Values and Choice of Charitable Cause: An Exploration of Donors' Giving Behaviour", *Nonprofit and Voluntary Sector Quarterly* 49 (4), 803–826.

Sudbury, A. and Vossler, C. (2022) "Checking Out Checkout Charity: A Study of Point-of-Sale Donation Campaigns", *Journal of Economic Behaviour and Organisation* 204, 252–270.

Thomas, S., Kureshi, S. and Vatavwala, S. (2020) "Cause-Related Marketing Research (1988–2016): An Academic Review and Classification", *Journal of Nonprofit and Public Sector Marketing* 32 (5), 488–516.

Varadarajan, P. and Menon A. (1988) "Cause Related Marketing: A Coalignment of Marketing Strategy and Corporate Philanthropy", *Journal of Marketing* 52 (3), 58–74.

Webb, D., Green, C. and Brashear, T. (2000) "Development and Validation of Scales to Measure Attitudes Influencing Monetary Donations to Charitable Organizations", *Journal of the Academy of Marketing Science* 28 (2), 299–309.

White, K., Poulson, B. and Hyde, M. (2016) "Identity and Personality Influences on Donating Money, Time and Blood", *Nonprofit and Voluntary Sector Quarterly* 46 (2), 372–394.

Wiepking, P. (2007) "The Philanthropic Poor: In Search of Explanations for the Relative Generosity of Lower Income Households", *Voluntas* 18, 339–358.

Wiepking, P. (2010) "Democrats Support International Relief and the Upper Class Donates to Art: How Opportunity, Incentives and Confidence Affect Donations to Different Types of Charitable Organisations", *Social Science Research* 39, 1073–1087.

Williams, R. (2003) "Women on Corporate Boards of Directors and Their Influence on Corporate Philanthropy", *Journal of Business Ethics* 42 (1), 1–10.

Williamson, G. and Clark, M. (1989) "Providing Help and Desired Relationship Type as Determinants of Changes in Self-evaluations", *Journal of Personality and Social Psychology* 56 (7), 722–734.

Wymer, W., Becker, A., and Boenigk, S. (2021) "The Antecedents of Charity Trust and Its Influence on Charity Supportive Behavior". *International Journal of Nonprofit and Voluntary Sector Marketing* 26, e1690, 1–11.

Wymer, W. and Samu S. (2003) *Nonprofit and Business Sector Collaboration*, New York: Haworth Press.

Ye, N., Teng, L., Yu. Y. and Wang, Y. (2015) "What's in it for Me? The Effect of Donation Outcomes on Donation Behaviour", *Journal of Business Research* 68 (3), 480–486.

Zhao, Q., Chen, C., Wang, J. and Chen, P. (2017) "Determinants' of Backers Funding Intention in Crowdfunding: Social Exchange Theory and Regulatory Focus", *Telematics and Informatics* 34, 370–384.

3 Fundraising in theory and practice

This chapter focuses on theories and practices regarding the need to *retain* as well as attract supporters and on research concerning the marketing practices (notably advertising and branding) that nonprofits employ to induce members of the public to want to engage with a fundraising organisation. Donor retention is closely associated with the application of 'relationship marketing' by nonprofits and with the various theories (e.g., Dialogic Theory, Social Judgement Theory) and research approaches (e.g., discourse analysis) that relationship marketing has been posited to involve. Thus, relationship marketing is the first topic explored below. Problems associated with relationship marketing are outlined, including the issues of 'slacktivism' and 'unprofitable' donors. The roles of nonprofit advertising and branding are then discussed.

Nonprofit relationship marketing

Boenigk's (2014) introduction to the International Journal of Nonprofit and Voluntary Sector Marketing's Special Issue on *Innovative Nonprofit Relationship Marketing* (Vol. 19 [2]) defined nonprofit relationship marketing as 'all strategies and instruments to systematically recruit, retain, and/or reactivate new or lost donors' (p. 53). Activities employed by nonprofits engaged in relationship marketing include telemarketing, database marketing, relationship advertising (see below), mailings of promotional materials, the sale of charity-branded products and memorabilia, and 'bonding' events such as open days or gala dinners. These (and other) activities are intended to develop a donor's sense of shared values and affiliation with a nonprofit and to invoke deep levels of organisational attachment among the nonprofit's supporters. Mato-Santiso, Rey-García, and Sanzo-Pérez (2021) observed how contemporary nonprofit organisations need to maintain effective relationships with an increasing multiplicity of stakeholders and that the various stakeholders had potentially divergent interests. However, developments in digital technology had enabled interactions with stakeholders to take place through multiple channels. The authors' review of 169 peer-reviewed articles in the field identified four major clusters of literature. Cluster one contained articles that

DOI: 10.4324/9781003364405-3

described how social media provided cost-effective interactivity opportunities. Articles in clusters two and three explained how the use of online tools and channels could improve fundraising and cause advocacy. Research reported in cluster four examined the channels and tools that nonprofits employed to engage stakeholders, both online (websites and social media) and offline (cause-related events and charity retailing).

Academic interest in nonprofit relationship marketing grew sharply following the appearance of Burnett's (1992) seminal text *Relationship Fundraising*, which reported the essential differences between nonprofit relationship fundraising and 'transactional' fundraising. The latter aimed at securing 'one-off' donations, provided ad hoc information and limited services to donors, had a short-term perspective, was arm's length and impersonal, and focused on attracting as many donors as possible without subsequent attempts to follow up contacts. Relationship fundraising, on the other hand, sought to establish long-term relationships with carefully segmented individuals and employed customised information useful for satisfying donors' needs. Today, many nonprofits invest heavily in relationship marketing due, *inter alia*, to the realisation that it is considerably cheaper to retain and satisfy existing donors than it is to acquire fresh supporters. (Normally, the up-front cost of procuring a supporter exceeds the financial value of the person's contributions during the first year of a relationship.) Also, wastage rates among donors are high (typically between 10% and 20% annually of all people who make more than one contribution). Thus, around half of all the individuals who give to a charity more than once are likely to disappear every three to five years.

Wastage rates are especially high among donors recruited face to face. An important article that investigated this particular issue was that of Sargeant and Hudson (2007), who reported 50% annual attrition rates among a sample of donors who had been recruited in this way. Sargeant and Hudson (2007) surveyed 1,000 active and 900 lapsed donors with the aim of establishing the main factors behind lapsed donors' decisions to stop giving. The findings indicated that the primary influences on lapse decisions were (i) financial pressures, (ii) wanting to switch support to an alternative nonprofit, (iii) changes in personal priorities, and (iv) wanting to support a nonprofit by means other than through financial donations. A subsequent study of a related problem, i.e., that of recently recruited donors switching their allegiance to an alternative nonprofit, was undertaken by Bennett (2009) who found that the major influences on switch decisions were the 'better congruence' of the second nonprofit's cause with a donor's interests and values, a person's boredom and overfamiliarity with the first nonprofit's communications, and the attractiveness of the second nonprofit's campaigns. An individual's innate desire for variation was also associated with switch decisions.

A number of researchers have sought to develop theoretical frameworks to explain the adoption of nonprofit relationship marketing activities. McAllister (2013), for instance, employed Dialogic Theory to analyse the websites of

19 fundraising educational establishments. Dialogic Theory proposes that 'meaning' is best understood via dialogue as occurs in two-way conversation. Dialogue should be egalitarian, McAllister (2013) argued, with neither party dominating. This requires good listening skills on both sides. Information provided should be based on valid claims. Therefore, the author suggested, nonprofits must 'foster an air of open dialogue with the public' (p. 24) and treat the donating public as an equal in communications. McAllister (2013) examined the 19 websites in terms of their ease of interface, usefulness of information, and presence of feedback loops (e.g., chat lines, blogs, discussion forums). Results were mixed, with many fundraising nonprofits in the sample not following the principles of dialogic communication. Websites needed to be open, honest, and forthcoming, McAllister (2013) insisted.

In a similar vein, Smitko (2012) used discourse analysis (which in the present context relates to the analysis of language and language structures occurring within conversations between nonprofits and donors) in order to examine the textual construction of tweets and responses to tweets that the author collected in case studies of two nonprofit organisations. The study searched for patterns of two-way conversations and found that, through Twitter, a participatory culture grew online and that this culture of participation facilitated strong relationships and produced strong donor engagement with the two nonprofits. The tweets sent by the nonprofits emphasised an organisation's credibility, frequently included emotional appeals, and often used logical reasoning. Interestingly, Smitko (2012) concluded that Social Judgement Theory and Social Networking Theory *emerged* as driving forces behind the author's results. Social Judgement Theory involves self-persuasion through a person perceiving and evaluating a suggestion by comparing it with the individual's current attitudes. Social Networking Theory relates to the manners whereby the social structures around a person affect beliefs and behaviour. The strategies employed by nonprofits when tweeting to supporters appeared to involve message linking activities (retweets, mentions, etc.) that were especially apposite to Social Network Theory, although Social Judgement Theory also seemed to be relevant to the author's data, because individuals appeared to evaluate an organisation's tweets according to how the tweets related to their current attitudes. Another useful paper dealing specifically with online relationship marketing was that of Lucas (2017), who investigated how the UK's three largest charities used Facebook to encourage social interactions among both actual and potential supporters. Facebook was employed by the organisations to 'humanise the brand' and to foster feelings of obligation. These objectives were achieved through the application of three strategies, i.e., publicly recognising individual supporters, projecting an organisational image of authority, and inculcating a sense of self-efficacy among supporters.

Methods for cultivating relationships with donors in general (not exclusively online) were discussed by Waters (2009) in an article that reported the outcomes to a survey of 1,830 donors to three nonprofit hospitals. The research aimed to establish managers' and donors' views about relationship cultivation techniques. Specifically, the research applied a 'co-orientation' methodology to assess the degrees of agreement that occurred between the managers of the three hospitals and its donors concerning the importance of various 'cultivation strategies' prominent in theories of interpersonal communication. The main strategies considered were: 'access', i.e., an organisation's willingness to make its people available to donors (e.g., via chat lines and discussion forums); 'positivity', i.e., a nonprofit's attempts to create positive experiences for donors; 'openness', i.e., the provision of honest and direct information and discussion; and 'assurance', i.e., an organisation's commitment to maintaining relationships with donors. Another interesting contribution to discussions about relationship cultivation was Alborough's (2017) finding that, very often, donors' long-term relationships with nonprofits mainly involved their relationships with *individual* fundraisers within organisations, rather than with an organisation itself. This conclusion was based on interviews conducted by the author with 44 senior managers and fundraisers in 14 nonprofits examining the details of 'primary relationships' with supporters. The results of the interviews suggested that the efforts of individual fundraisers created a narrative that caused donors to feel both cared for by an organisation and connected with its work. This resulted in supporters wanting to engage in reciprocal relationships.

MacQuillin, Sargeant, and Shang (2016) argued that Psychological Identity Theory could offer a suitable framework for determining how fundraising nonprofits can create long-term relationships with donors. Psychological Identity Theory relates to self-image, self-esteem, and individuality. Self-evaluations of these properties are based on an individual's qualities, beliefs, emotions, thought patterns, personality, and self-expressions. The theory posits that choices and commitments are made according to a personal psychological identity. Thus, MacQuillin et al. (2016) opined, it might be possible to cultivate a sense of psychological identity among donors that involves a supported organisation. Hence, it may be feasible to build communal (not transactional) relationships with donors who possess a psychological self-identity that includes the organisation in question. MacQuillin et al. (2016) also noted the potential role of Privacy Regulation Theory (which concerns people's desires to exert selective control over social interactions and to plan interactions with others) in helping a fundraising nonprofit to determine optimum contact levels and frequencies with donors. The authors further noted the potential relevance for relationship fundraising of Self-Determination Theory, i.e., the notion that donors, in order to feel that they have lived a fulfilled life, believe that they must offer gifts to others. This might cause donors to want close relationships with causes they like and to make informed choices when offering support.

Box 3.1 Research opportunities: relationship marketing

Relationship fundraising has been the subject of extensive investigation. Useful future research in the field could focus on connections between relationship fundraising and the introduction of new technologies, particularly those connected to Big Data and the latest data mining techniques, as discussed in Chapters 4 and 5. Big Data will facilitate the identification and targeting of high lifetime-value prospective donors and will improve income forecasts, hence helping to plan relationship marketing strategies. Studies of fundraising managers' knowledge of these new technologies and states of readiness for their application would be worthwhile. Scope remains, moreover, for research into the effectiveness of relationship fundraising vis-à-vis donor retention and levels of giving, and also into the impacts of the annoyance and irritation that materials related to relationship fundraising can cause. Adaptations of pre-existing scales that have already been employed to measure irritation and annoyance in the commercial sector could be useful in assessing the consequences of these emotions among donors to nonprofits.

Unprofitable donors

Relationships with some donors are more profitable than relationships with others. This is because relationship fundraising activities can attract large numbers of low-value donors who, while giving very little, are expensive to service. The propensity of relationship fundraising to attract large numbers of unprofitable donors who make very small and infrequent gifts, but who thereafter receive expensive materials (welcome packs, catalogues, newsletters, etc.), is a problematic issue that all fundraisers engaging in relationship marketing need to address. The cost of servicing small donors is substantial, given that the amount of resources required to process a small donation is about the same as that needed to process a large gift. Noting that fundraising nonprofits commonly implement 'donor priority strategies' (i.e., strategies that deliberately provide favourable treatment to higher value donors), Boenigk and Scherhag (2014) investigated the question of how the prioritisation of certain donor groups might affect donor satisfaction and loyalty. The authors surveyed 804 donors to a certain fundraising nonprofit which deliberately differentiated its service provision between 'high' and 'low' donors. Findings from the study revealed that the organisation's priority strategy encouraged higher level donors to give more *and* encouraged lower-level donors to upgrade their contributions. In conclusion, the authors recommended that fundraisers operate service differentiation policies in order to achieve this sort of beneficial result, but with just a few donor differentiation levels.

Sauve-Rodd (2007) analysed the financial records of 72,000 supporters of a single charity, finding that half of all the donors in the charity's database were unprofitable in any one year. Moreover, 75% of the charity's profit (defined as total revenue from donors minus the total cost of servicing them) came from just 10% of the organisation's supporters. The situation was partly attributable, Sauve-Rodd (2007) claimed, to mass market relationship fundraising campaigns that attracted large numbers of non-monthly donors (i.e., people who had not agreed to monthly bank or payroll standing orders in favour of the charity) who instead made single small value gifts. Such donors were not worth retaining, Sauve-Rodd (2007) suggested. Another difficulty was that fundraisers often measured the profitability of specific campaigns or activities and not the profitability of individual donors. Assessing the profitability of a particular donor segment was inappropriate, Sauve-Rodd (2007) continued, because the result would be an average value that disguised the presence of individual unprofitable supporters.

The problem of small and infrequent donors reducing the profitability of relationship fundraising activities can be exacerbated if a relationship fundraising campaign attracts 'slacktivists', characterised by Kristofferson, White, and Peloza (2014) as people who will make a small donation to a good cause in order to fulfil their altruistic self-perceptions, yet fail to make further gifts or make gifts of very low value. Often a slacktivist will donate online, and perhaps join a Facebook nonprofit support group and/or participate in other relationships with a nonprofit. However, the person's donor lifetime value will be low. Two primary motives lay behind slacktivism, Kristofferson et al. (2014) opined, i.e., a desire to present a positive image to others, and an internal need to be consistent with personal values. The authors noted that the research evidence on whether slacktivists can be developed into longer-term and more substantial supporters has been mixed, although studies have revealed that a high degree of 'observability' of the initial token gift made by a slacktivist appears to lead to higher subsequent donations. Another means for helping to deal with the problem of small ad hoc donations not actually leading to longer-term and more substantial support was proposed by Khodakarami, Peterson, and Venkatesan (2015), who suggested 'donation variety' as a way of developing long-term relationships with newly acquired donors. People who interacted with a nonprofit by participating in a very broad range of activities would, according to Khodakarami et al. (2015), often turn out to be profitable in the longer run. Therefore, a nonprofit should provide new donors with numerous opportunities to interact in disparate ways with the organisation.

Deciding how best to deal with unprofitable donors is a vexing issue that was addressed directly by Bennett and Kottasz (2011), who examined the methods used to deal with unprofitable donors applied by a sample of 195 UK fundraising charities. The sample organisations reported that, on the average, 31% of their supporters were unprofitable. One in eight of the charities formally deselected unprofitable donors by removing them from their databases entirely. Nearly half of the organisations reduced the volumes of materials despatched to unprofitable donors, and a further quarter applied other measures, e.g., sending cheaper and lower quality materials. The authors identified a number of factors that significantly influenced the probability that a charity would *avoid* deselecting unprofitable donors, namely, the extent to which a charity engaged in relationship marketing; the organisation's level of market orientation (which exerted a negative effect); the charity's 'psychological closeness' to its donors; 'organisational inertia'; and beliefs that unprofitable donors were likely to become profitable in the future.

Further difficulties apply to relationship marketing in addition to the possibility of attracting unprofitable donors. Investments in relationship marketing carry opportunity costs. Donors to nonprofits might not *want* relationships with the organisations they support. Even the most faithful supporters of charitable organisations may become weary of being deluged with relationship marketing campaign materials and communications. These (and other) considerations have induced researchers to examine nonprofit organisations' attempts at securing donor *engagement* as a means for inducing longer-term and stronger relationships with supporters. Bennett (2013) created a 16-item donor engagement scale to examine this matter. Donor engagement was defined as a donor's behaviour towards a nonprofit that went well beyond the mere act of giving and was likely to extend to word-of-mouth referrals, volunteering, and/ or otherwise participating in the organisation's activities, joining and interacting with communities (especially online communities) that support a cause,

---

Box 3.2   Research opportunities: donor engagement

Although the topic of *customer* engagement has been researched extensively within the commercial sector, and while nonprofit donor engagement has featured prominently in the grey literature on nonprofit fundraising, little research has been undertaken into donor engagement in the academic marketing domain. Thus, many research opportunities arise relating to this subject. What are the best donor engagement strategies to apply in various circumstances? How should the effectiveness of donor engagement strategies be measured? What are the best communication channels to use in order to attain engagement? At what point in the donor journey is a person likely to become engaged, and why? What events and experiences might destroy a donor's sense of engagement with a nonprofit?

blogging, web posting, advocacy, and purchasing a nonprofit's merchandise. (Purchase of merchandise might actually increase even though donations to a nonprofit may be decreasing over time.) An engaged donor would feel highly involved and intimate with the nonprofit, and (critically) these sensations would be experienced in the long term. Bennett's (2013) donor engagement scale contained sections for donor 'enthusiasm', 'passion', and deep 'interest' in a charitable organisation's work. All three of these dimensions were found to relate significantly to levels of financial donation. The study also revealed that donors who regarded a nonprofit's relationship marketing activities as 'excellent' were more likely than others to (i) engage with the organisation, (ii) perceive their overall relationships with the nonprofit to be of high quality, and (iii) give more generously and frequently.

Advertising by fundraising nonprofits

Advertising has the potential to contribute to relationship marketing because advertisements can be crafted to offer representations of reality that imitate relationships. Thus, the content and form of an advertisement can be arranged in ways that stimulate thoughts, feelings, and actions relevant to a relationship and which consequently influence a potential donor's assessments of the desirability of entering, remaining with, or leaving a relationship with a nonprofit. In general, advertising on television, on social media, and in the press is one of the most important fundraising tools available to a nonprofit. Academic research on nonprofit advertising has been extensive. Often research has focused on how fundraising advertisements are framed (see below), particularly vis-à-vis the portrayal of a nonprofit's beneficiaries. Research has also examined the effectiveness of various layouts and wordings of advertisements. An interesting illustration of research involving nonprofit advertisement design was an investigation completed by Choi, Rangan, and Singh (2016) that explored the effects on donor behaviour of including cold images (ice, freezing winter scenarios, etc.) in fundraising advertisements. It emerged that study participants who had been exposed to pictures of cold objects experienced feelings of physical coldness, which in turn led to perceptions of loneliness. Therefore, the authors concluded, negative emotional appeals in advertisements (i.e., those showing victims' distress, suffering, etc., intended to provoke shock and anger among audiences) that people view *after* seeing cold images will be less effective for eliciting donations.

Most readers will be familiar with nonprofit advertisements broadcast on television or contained in appeals sent by mail or email wherein the organisation asks for a donation of a specific amount. Advertisements of this nature typically contain phrases such as 'Give just £XX and you will feed a starving child in war-torn XXX for XX days'. The research question concerning such solicitations is the determination of exactly how much money the nonprofit should ask the viewer to give. Academic studies addressing this matter have often used Assimilation-Contrast Theory to offer solutions. Assimilation-Contrast Theory suggests that information that is in accord with a person's own beliefs and attitudes is more likely to be accepted. The amount proposed in a solicitation will act as an anchor, i.e., an external reference point that is intended to 'nudge' donors into giving the stated amount. Assimilation-Contrast Theory posits that donors compare the reference point against their current beliefs regarding how much they should give. If the amount suggested by the nonprofit is credible and congruent with a person's beliefs, the suggested amount is 'assimilated' and this amount is donated. De Bruyn and Prokopec (2017) noted how Assimilation-Contrast Theory had been tested many times in laboratory experiments, but with mixed and frequently contradictory results. Hence, the authors conducted a field experiment on 23,500 supporters of a single nonprofit whereby some of the sample members were sent an appeal for a donation that was a little higher in value than the amount of the individual's previous donation to the nonprofit (as recorded in the organisation's database), while the remainder of the sample was sent an appeal for a donation of exactly the same amount as the person's previous donation. Asking for the higher amount increased average donations by 22%.

Framing of fundraising advertisements

Framing an advertisement involves deciding on the format of its executional components, e.g., the headline, pictures, body copy, and layout. Advertisements can be framed positively or negatively, with the intention of arousing particular thoughts and feelings among the people who see them. A comprehensive and valuable review of literature on the framing of fundraising advertisements is contained in a paper by Das, Kerkhof, and Kuiper (2008). As well as reviewing past literature on the subject, the authors conducted an experimental study which found that the provision of 'abstract' information within nonprofit advertisements (defined by the authors as information presented as statistics) was more effective when combined with a negatively framed message, whereas anecdotal ('vivid') messages were more effective when combined with a positively framed message. A positively framed message was described as one seeking to invoke pleasant thoughts within viewers or readers by showing a nonprofit's magnificent work and the excellent consequences of this work for the organisation's beneficiaries. An interesting extension of this line of research was provided by Laufer, Silvera, McBride, and Schertzer (2010) who examined the effects of different types of framing of nonprofit advertisements that had been shown in countries with different cultures. Consequent to experiments conducted in the USA and Mexico, the authors concluded that a nonprofit's ability to communicate its 'success stories' would depend on the cultural context (individualistic or collectivist) in which the organisation operated.

The effectiveness of 'gain-framed' versus 'loss-framed' charity advertisements was investigated by Xu and Huang (2020) in a meta-analysis of 27 studies, concluding that gain-framed and loss-framed appeals do not differ significantly with respect to the persuasiveness of appeals. Gain-framed messages emphasise positive outcomes (e.g., 'With your donation, you will save a child'). Loss-framed appeals highlight negative consequences (e.g., 'Without your donation, a child will go to bed hungry'). This result was confirmed by a systematic literature review of 63 articles on charity advertising completed by Wymer and Gross (2021) who concluded that prior research on the use of negative or positive framing was less important than an advertisement's capacity to evoke sympathy for beneficiaries. Sympathy was aroused most effectively via the application of altruistic (rather than egoistic) appeals.

A great deal of criticism has been directed against both (i) the ways in which fundraising nonprofits frame their advertisements and (ii) the specific contents of advertisements published by fundraising organisations. Criticisms typically involve assertions that fundraising advertisements (i) are excessively emotional; (ii) appear too frequently; (iii) use actors to portray victims rather than using real victims of illnesses, disasters, etc.; (iv) are expensive and divert a nonprofit organisation's resources away from its core mission; and (v) may be counterproductive through arousing 'compassion fatigue' among viewers. (The term 'compassion fatigue' refers to the numbing effect on members of the public of incessant media exposure to images of suffering, resulting in people becoming desensitised to the distress of victims.) Responses to these criticisms include the arguments that heavily emotive advertisements (i) are usually effective for 'opening the public purse', (ii) realistically highlight the desperate needs of victims, and (iii) have the capacity to act as 'moral education' for viewers and readers.

Guilt appeals

An aspect of negative framing that has attracted considerable attention is the attempt by fundraisers to arouse in viewers' minds feelings of guilt at not donating. Advertisements with pictures of emaciated and disease-ridden children, of starving animals, pathetic victims of disasters, etc., and which are accompanied by textual messages stating that 'these people/animals will die/ continue suffering if you do not donate' are often used by charities. Guilt-based appeals have been criticised for causing distress and anxiety among sensitively minded viewers. Nevertheless, research has generally found guilt-inducing messages to be an effective method for raising funds. This was confirmed in empirical work completed by Hibbert, Smith, Davies, and Ireland (2007), which concluded that guilt arousal in nonprofit advertisements was positively associated with both donation intention and donors' favourable beliefs about a nonprofit. Moreover, Hibbert et al. (2007) argued, persuasive tactics could be used by a nonprofit to manipulate the number of guilty feelings generated by a particular advertisement. A similar outcome was obtained in research undertaken by Basil, Ridgway, and Basil (2008), who developed a model to explore possible connections between empathy, self-efficacy (meaning, in the present context, a person's belief in the individual's ability to do something about the problem depicted in an advertisement), and donation intention. Their results indicated that people strong in both empathy and self-efficacy experienced high levels of guilt when confronted with a guilt appeal, and this in turn shaped donation intention. Empathy fully mediated the connection between empathy and donation intention, while self-efficacy partially mediated the relationship. Chang (2014) also sought to explain the mechanisms through which guilt can influence people's responses to nonprofit advertisements. The author created an 'affect forecasting and regulation model', which showed how negative feelings of guilt aroused by an advertisement could be partially assuaged by including within the advertisement an egoistically orientated (rather than an altruistic) appeal. This was because egoistic messages strengthened viewers' beliefs that giving would lead to their feeling good about themselves.

Psychologists make an important distinction between 'guilt' and 'shame' since, although these words are often used interchangeably, they constitute quite different constructs. Allegedly, guilt engenders a sense of responsibility, whereas shame may give rise to feelings of having done something dishonourable and/or improper by not acting in a particular way. Research into the guilt/shame divide is regularly reported in the social marketing literature (for reviews, see, for example, Agrawal and Duhachek [2010] and Brennan and Binney [2010]) but is scarce within the nonprofit marketing domain. However, Xu (2022) examined the impacts of guilt and shame in charity advertising via two studies, the first of which comprised a survey that investigated the extent to which anticipatory guilt and shame affected people's purchase intentions relating to a cause-related product. Study 2 involved an experiment that examined the effects of guilt versus shame appeals on the ways in which charity-advertising messages were cognitively processed. Results from each of the investigations indicated that both anticipatory guilt and ad-induced guilt connected positively and significantly with behavioural intentions. Participants with higher interdependent self-construal were more likely to exhibit charitable behaviours. Anticipatory shame was positively connected with behavioural intention, but this was not the case for ad-induced shame. Also, self-construal negatively moderated the effect of shame. The impact of anticipatory shame on behavioural intentions was stronger among people with higher independent self-construal.

Images of beneficiaries

Another frequently criticised aspect of the advertisements of some nonprofit organisations concerns the employment within advertisements of pictures of a nonprofit's (human) beneficiaries that arguably demean and improperly stereotype the people involved, especially beneficiaries who reside in Third World countries. Examples are pictures of naked, starving children with bloated bellies and helpless and bewildered adults dressed in rags and living in shanty towns. Such advertisements have been dubbed 'poverty porn' by the news media. Advertisements of this type allegedly create unpleasant 'begging bowl' stereotypes of beneficiaries, infantilise and degrade the individuals portrayed, and reinforce the idea of the superiority of the northern hemisphere over the south (see Cameron and Haanstra [2008] for a review of literature concerning these matters). Moreover, advertisements of this type often use either paid actors in studio settings or complicit and paid local people in the pictures that appear in appeals; they do not use individuals who were actually affected by the catastrophe or health condition depicted. The ethics of the organisations producing these images were examined by Ong (2015). Advertisements containing 'shock effect' images of this nature could go too far, Ong (2015) suggested, could dehumanise victims of a disaster (a typhoon hitting the Philippines in the author's particular case), and had the capacity to create compassion fatigue among donors. Yet, Ong (2015) continued, these pictures could open the eyes of viewers to the tragedy involved and (via the arousal of vicarious distress) could activate compassion leading to positive donation decisions. A useful study regarding the mass media's use of images of people in distress was Bhati and Eikenberry's (2016) investigation of how destitute children in India *themselves* felt about how they were represented in nonprofit fundraising advertisements. It emerged that the children participating in the study liked to be portrayed in a good light and as being 'happy' with life. Equally, they wanted to be shown in ways that told the whole story of their lives, including the extreme hardships they faced. The children interviewed knew they had been photographed but did not know how their images were going to be used in fundraising advertisements. Bhati (2021) queried whether representations by International Nongovernmental Organisations of people of colour who lived in developing nations stereotyped the individuals depicted. The author examined 320 photographs from the 32 largest such organisations operating in the United States. Results suggested that the organisations generally portrayed beneficiaries in stereotypical manners and thereby reinforced 'colonial' narratives. Single mothers, infants, and girls were heavily represented in pictures, but there were few representations of men and families.

The extant literature on shock tactics in nonprofit advertising in general was reviewed by Dahl (2018), who defined shock advertising as 'that which deliberately, rather than inadvertently, startles and offends its audiences by violating norms for social values and personal ideals' (p. 2). Dahl (2018) observed that most academic research on shock advertising had studied situations where an advertisement (real-life or specially created for an experiment) was either shocking or was not shocking and had ignored intermediate situations. Albouy (2017) addressed this matter through a study that employed three different levels of shock in experiments. The results showed that the more shocking the advertisement, the greater the degrees that both the empathy and the negative emotions (sadness, fear, and guilt) that were engendered by the advertisement led to positive attitudes towards (i) the advertisement itself, (ii) the cause depicted, and (iii) donation intention. Albouy's (2017) results demonstrated that a person's self-efficacy, involvement with a cause, and belief that a nonprofit was capable of solving beneficiaries' problems interacted with negative emotions to produce positive attitudes and intention to donate. The author attributed these results to Negative-State Relief Theory, which posits that the negative emotions experienced when a person is exposed to a shocking advertisement motivate the individual to give to the advertising nonprofit because donating is the quickest and most effective way of attenuating the unpleasant emotional state created by seeing the advertisement.

Box 3.3   Research opportunities: nonprofit advertising

Dahl's (2018) abovementioned review identified several areas for future research on the subject of shock fundraising advertisements. Would, for example, fundraising advertisements that are shocking in terms of profanity be equally or unequally effective as advertisements that are shocking in terms of violence or sex? Would such advertisements have the same effects for different types of cause, and if not, what would explain disparities? For how long should potential donors be exposed to a shock advertisement in order to optimise response taking into consideration the clutter of other advertisements surrounding the shock advertisement in question?

Nonprofit advertising is routinely criticised for producing excessively emotive and sometimes offensive advertisements. Research opportunities arise therefore in the exploration of this criticism. For example, what are the profiles of the people who are most offended, and how much and how often do they donate to nonprofits? If a particular donor is not offended by an advertisement, is the person's donation behaviour affected by knowing that other people have been offended? It would be interesting to investigate the accuracy of the representations contained in emotive advertisement, and whether the most accurate or the most inaccurate depictions of beneficiaries generate the highest levels of donations. Comments about a nonprofit's advertisements are written by journalists and monitored by the editors of publications. It would be useful to examine the perspectives on emotive nonprofit advertising held by media editors and individual journalists.

Branding of nonprofit organisations

Nonprofits were initially slow to adopt branding (due mainly to opposition from stakeholders, especially employees and trustees), but branding became widespread in the 1990s and is today practised by all the large and, in some form or other, by most small fundraising organisations. Branding increased in popularity because it enabled nonprofits to communicate their core values and operations to the donating public, to impel all the stakeholders of an organisation to deliver the same brand promise, and to demonstrate a nonprofit's 'professional' approach. The adoption of branding was accelerated by the observation among non-branded nonprofits that nonprofits that engaged in branding were achieving higher financial returns (see Stride, 2006, for information on this point). An early study of nonprofit (charity) branding completed by Tapp (1996) defined a charity's brand as 'the complete collection of images of a charity, its products or its cause, that are contained in a donor's mind' (p. 329). Tapp (1996) executed a qualitative investigation of attitudes towards branding that were held by senior marketing executives in large charities, concluding that although many of them used branding, they did not describe it as such. Often, brands had arisen through 'accident of circumstance' rather than in a planned manner (p. 329). Also, 'brand development' work was scarce. Some of the executives in Tapp's (1996) sample were wary of branding since, at the time, they believed that brand management by charities would not be accepted by a large section of the donating public. Therefore, the author suggested, both the donor community and the general public needed to be 're-educated about branding'. Tapp (1996) noted that the roots of brand management were in the commercial sector and that many of the people recruited into charity marketing had commercial sector backgrounds (bringing with them ideas and conceptual frameworks found in the for-profit sector). This could cause internal disputes about the direction a charity's brand development should take. Should fundraising be paramount or should a brand identity focus entirely on the organisation's cause? Bilgin and Kethüda (2022) examined, via a survey of 521 potential donors in Turkey, the extent to which charity social media marketing influenced charity brand image, brand trust, and donation intention. Charity social media marketing consisted of measures to develop awareness, interaction, timeliness, informativeness, and customisation. Only awareness had a significant direct impact on donation intention. Timeliness and informativeness significantly affected charity brand image, while brand trust was influenced by informativeness and customisation. Charity social media marketing as a whole affected donation intention both directly and indirectly through brand image and brand trust.

The issue of commercial thinking possibly influencing charity brand management was followed up by Stride (2006) who, in a study of UK charities, observed that because branding consultants tended to adopt for-profit approaches (manifest in the application of human personality adjectives to brands, emphasis on visual identities, logos, graphic design, etc.), the brand identities of many charities had become too broad, even meaningless. Examples of brand identities considered by Stride (2006) to be excessively broad included identities based on a charity being 'trustworthy, altruistic, or benevolent'. Brand identities of this nature failed to distinguish one charity from others. Rather, Stride (2006) argued, a charity's brand identity should be firmly rooted in its values and ideals, which should be non-negotiable and should not change over time. The practice of embedding values and ideals in brand identities could differentiate charities from commercial businesses, which routinely changed their brand identities as consumer opinion altered.

It is the case, nevertheless, that nonprofits do sometimes rebrand. Reasons for rebranding include changes in a nonprofit's vision and strategies, influences emanating from an organisation's marketing department, or a pressing need to attract more donations. Lee and Bourne (2017) examined, through a study of ten charities that had rebranded their identities, a number of issues connected with the internal tensions that could arise within charities due to rebranding. Conflicts were observed between, on the one hand, marketers in the ten charities and, on the other hand, stakeholders who did not want to relinquish established organisational identities. Nevertheless, pressures to secure financial resources often led to the adoption of new brand identities that possessed utilitarian themes. Sometimes, 'dual identities' existed within a charity: one emphasising a charity's traditional values, and the other driven by financial imperatives. Top management within a charity undergoing a rebranding exercise needed to justify the policy to all stakeholders, to communicate new visions, and to use all their managerial skills to reduce internal tensions.

Nonprofit brand personality and image

Attempts have been made to relate a nonprofit organisation's characteristics to human characteristics (genuine, strong, energetic, etc.) as a means for identifying the 'personality' of a nonprofit brand. Literature relating to this matter was reviewed comprehensively by Voeth and Herbst (2008), who also developed a nonprofit brand personality scale designed to measure the features of the brand personality of a nonprofit organisation. The authors' 36-item scale contained three components: (i) social competence and trust (which was assessed via 21 items, e.g., professional, trustworthy), (ii) emotion and assertiveness (11 items, e.g., exciting, courageous), and (iii) sophistication (five items, e.g., cheerful, glamourous). The scale was tested on donors' perceptions of three well-known nonprofits (UNICEF, Greenpeace, and the German Red Cross) and was found to be valid and reliable. In the same year, Sargeant, Ford, and Hudson (2008) presented another analysis of brand personality, which they tested in relation to nine national UK nonprofits. The authors concluded that the following traits distinguished one nonprofit brand from others: (i) emotional engagement (e.g., exciting, fun, inspiring), (ii) service (e.g., dedicated, compassionate), (iii) the nonprofit's 'tradition', and (iv) voice (e.g., ambitious, authoritative, bold). However, the following traits did not significantly discriminate among the organisations: benevolence, progression (i.e., a nonprofit's capacity to effect social change), and conservatism. Of all nonprofit brand personality traits, brand 'warmth' was found to be the most important in a study undertaken by Bernritter, Verlegh, and Smit (2016). Brand warmth predicted the ease with which nonprofit brands obtained 'likes' on Facebook. This in turn enabled a nonprofit to acquire online endorsements. Images of 'competence', conversely, did not result in 'likes' and endorsements. The warmth effect was enhanced by a brand's ability to communicate 'symbolic value' (i.e., the brand's capacity to state something positive about the person who was contemplating its characteristics) to an observer.

A paper by Bennett and Gabriel (2003) gave rise to a number of subsequent investigations concerning the components of a nonprofit's 'image'. Consequent to an empirical study, Bennett and Gabriel (2003) concluded that seven factors adequately explained public perceptions of a fundraising organisation's image, i.e., levels of compassion, dynamism and idealism; a focus on beneficiaries; being 'non-political'; and the organisation's reputation (e.g., for being well-managed) and 'popularity' (e.g., whether the nonprofit is well known). Michel and Rieunier (2012) criticised Bennett and Gabriel's (2003) scale on the grounds that it had been inspired by commercial business practices. Hence, Michel and Rieunier (2012) created a more compact scale for measuring a nonprofit's image and comprising just four dimensions: usefulness (e.g., indispensable, civic minded), efficiency (e.g., serious, well-managed), affect (e.g., warm, generous), and dynamism (e.g., modern, innovative). Application of this scale to samples of donors better explained donation intention than the scale proposed by Bennett and Gabriel (2003). Michel and Rieunier's (2012) scale was further tested, but in an online context, by Huang and Ku (2016) who explored relationships between the types of information displayed on nonprofit organisations' websites and their brand images. Huang and Ku (2016) concluded that disparate genres of information (e.g., goals and activities, news, organisational matters, financial statements) that were presented on websites did indeed exert different influences on website users' perceptions of a nonprofit's image. Information that generated images of dynamism and usefulness increased website viewers' intention to donate. The Michel and Rieunier (2012) scale was subjected to additional scrutiny by Michaelidou, Micevski, and Cadogan (2015), who then developed a six-factor scale with components for efficiency, usefulness, affect, dynamism, reliability, and ethicality, all of which significantly affected donation intention.

Brand orientation

A series of seminal papers by Hankinson (2000, 2001, 2002) explored the construct of 'brand orientation', defined by Hankinson (2000) as 'the extent

---

Box 3.4   Research opportunities: nonprofit branding

Research into nonprofit branding has been detailed and voluminous. Studies of nonprofit branding have tended to employ models derived from for-profit research and hence have focused on commercial managerial attitudes and approaches. Thus, research opportunities arise in respect of donors' and beneficiaries' opinions about branding practices. What, for example, is the influence on donors' and beneficiaries' attitudes and intentions of a nonprofit's position in published 'league tables' of charities? Do 'spill-over effects' apply to donors' and beneficiaries' perceptions of nonprofit brands, i.e., if the brand image of one organisation in a particular sector suddenly improves does this automatically enhance the brand images of other nonprofits in the same sector? Do stakeholders feel a genuine sense of pride in a nonprofit's brand image; if so, why and how does brand pride become manifest in stakeholders' behaviour?

As regards research relating to brand management, investigations are needed into the branding practices of micro-fundraising nonprofits, i.e., organisations run by just two or three people. What are the possibilities for joint branding by two or more organisations, some small and some large, for special projects (as occurs with the UK Disasters Emergency Committee for instance). Further topics for valuable research into nonprofit branding include (i) detailed investigations of connections between a nonprofit's brand and the organisation's susceptibility to experience mission drift (e.g., how to alter a brand image successfully after mission drift has occurred) and (ii) examinations of why some nonprofits decide not to develop a discernible brand. Yet, another interesting area for future research is an examination of the antecedents and consequences of 'brand visibility' and also whether high brand visibility causes a nonprofit to become vulnerable to adverse publicity. This question might be especially salient vis-à-vis the branding of nonprofits that deal with 'unpopular' causes.

---

to which charitable organisations regard themselves as brands'. Hankinson's initial investigation of 15 charities across 5 sectors revealed that the importance of branding was recognised by managers in the sample organisations and was seen as being particularly useful for raising awareness, for general fundraising, for building trust, and for lobbying politicians. However, little strategic brand management was evident in the charities studied. Hankinson (2001) extended this work via the construction of a conceptual framework to explain brand orientation. The antecedents of the framework were posited to comprise (i) a supportive organisational culture, (ii) the chief executive's personal vision, and (iii) a charity's experience of branding. As a result of this study, Hankinson (2001) characterised brand orientation in terms of four elements: understanding the brand, communicating the brand, employing the brand as a strategic resource, and managing the brand deliberately and actively. In 2002, Hankinson completed a quantitative study of brand orientation on managerial practice, finding that fundraising managers who were high in brand orientation attracted significantly more voluntary (but not statutory) income than others (Hankinson, 2002).

References

Agrawal, N. and Duhachek, A. (2010) "Emotional Compatibility and the Effectiveness of Antidrinking Messages: A Defensive Processing Perspective on Shame and Guilt", *Journal of Marketing Research* 47 (2), 263–273.

Alborough, L. (2017) "Lost in Translation: A Sociological Study of the Role of Fundraisers in Mediating Gift Giving in Nonprofit Organisations", *International Journal of Nonprofit and Voluntary Sector Marketing* 22 (4), e1602.

Albouy, J. (2017) "Emotions and Prosocial Behaviours: A Study of the Effectiveness of Shocking Advertising Campaigns", *Recherche et Applications en Marketing* 32 (2), 4–25.

Basil, D., Ridgway, N. and Basil, M. (2008) "Guilt and Giving: A Process Model of Empathy and Efficiency", *Psychology and Marketing* 25 (1), 1–23.

Bennett, R. (2009) "Factors Influencing Donor Switching Behaviour Among Charity Supporters: An Empirical Investigation", *Journal of Customer Behaviour* 8 (4), 329–345.

Bennett, R. (2013) "Elements, Causes and Effects of Donor Engagement Among Supporters of UK Charities", *International Review on Public and Nonprofit Marketing* 10 (3), 201–220.

Bennett, R. and Gabriel, H. (2003) "Image and Reputational Characteristics of UK Charitable Organisations: An Empirical Study", *Corporate Reputation Review* 6 (3), 276–289.

Bennett, R. and Kottasz, R. (2011) "Management of Unprofitable Donors by UK Fundraising Charities", *Journal of Customer Behaviour* 10 (4), 309–333.

Bernritter, S., Verlegh, P. and Smit, E. (2016) "Why Nonprofits are Easier to Endorse on Social Media: The Roles of Warmth and Brand Symbolism", *Journal of Interactive Marketing* 33, 27–42.

Bhati, A. (2021) "Is the Representation of Beneficiaries by International Nongovernmental Organizations (INGOs) Still Pornographic?", *Journal of Philanthropy and Marketing* Early View, 1–12.

Bhati, A. and Eikenberry, A. (2016) "Faces of the Needy: The Portrayal of Destitute Children in the Fundraising Campaigns of NGOs in India", *International Journal of Nonprofit and Voluntary Sector Marketing* 21 (1), 31–42.

Bilgin, Y. and Kethüda, Ö. (2022) "Charity Social Media Marketing and Its Influence on Charity Brand Image, Brand Trust, and Donation Intention", *Voluntas* 33, 1091–1102.

Boenigk, S. (2014) "Introduction to the Special Issue on Innovative Nonprofit Marketing", *International Journal of Nonprofit and Voluntary Services Marketing* 19 (2), 53–56.

Boenigk, S. and Scherhag, C. (2014) "Effects of Donor Priority Strategy on Relationship Fundraising Outcomes", *Nonprofit Management and Leadership* 24 (3), 307–336.

Brennan, L. and Binney, W. (2010) "Fear, Guilt and Shame Appeals in Social Marketing", *Journal of Business Research* 63 (2), 140–146.

Burnett, K. (1992) *Relationship Fundraising*, London: White Lion Press.

Cameron, J. and Haanstra, A. (2008) "Development Made Sexy: How it Happened and What It Means", *Third World Quarterly* 29 (8), 1475–1489.

Chang, C. (2014) "Guilt Regulation: The Relative Effects of Altruistic versus Egoistic Appeals for Charity Advertising", *Journal of Advertising* 43 (3), 211–227.

Choi, J., Rangan, P. and Singh, S. (2016) "Do Cold Images Cause Cold-heartedness? The Impact of Negative Emotional Charity Appeals", *Journal of Advertising* 45 (4), 417–425.

Dahl, D. (2018) "Shock Charity Campaigns: Building our Understanding on Their Effectiveness", *Recherche et Applications en Marketing* 33 (1), 88–91.

Das, E., Kerkhof, P. and Kuiper, J. (2008) "Improving the Effectiveness of Fundraising Messages: The Impact of Charity Goal Attainment, Message Framing and Evidence on Persuasion", *Journal of Applied Communication Research* 36 (2), 161–175.

De Bruyn, A. and Prokapec, S. (2017) "Assimilation-Contrast Theory in Action: Operationalisation and Managerial Impact in a Fundraising Context", *International Journal of Research in Marketing* 34 (2), 367–381.

Hankinson, P. (2000) "Brand Orientation in the Charity Sector: Qualitative Research into Key Charity Sectors", *International Journal of Nonprofit and Voluntary Sector Marketing* 5 (3), 207–219.

Hankinson, P. (2001) "Brand Orientation in the Charity Sector: A Framework for Discussion and Research", *International Journal of Nonprofit and Voluntary Sector Marketing* 6 (3), 231–242.

Hankinson, P. (2002) "The Impact of Brand Orientation on Managerial Practice: A Quantitative Study of the UK's Top 500 Fundraising Managers", *International Journal of Nonprofit and Voluntary Sector Marketing* 7 (1), 30–44.

Hibbert, S., Smith, A., Davies, A. and Ireland, F. (2007) "Guilt Appeals: Persuasion, Knowledge and Charitable Giving", *Psychology and Marketing* 24 (8), 723–742.

Huang, S. and Ku, H. (2016) "Brand Management for Nonprofit Organisations: Exploring the Relations Between Websites, Brand Images and Donations", *Journal of Electronic Commerce Research* 17 (1), 80–96.

Khodakarami, F., Peterson, J. and Venkatesan, (2015), "Developing Donor Relationships: The Role of Breadth of Giving", *Journal of Marketing* 79 (4), 77–93.

Kristofferson, K., White, K. and Peloza, J. (2014) "The nature of Slacktivism: How the Social Observability of an Initial Act of Token Support Affects Subsequent Prosocial Action", *Journal of Consumer Research* 40 (6), 1149–1166.

Laufer, D., Silvera, D., McBride, B. and Schertzer, S. (2010) "Communicating Charity Success Stories Across Cultures: Highlighting Individual or Collective Achievement", *European Journal of Marketing* 44 (9/10), 1322–1333.

Lee, Z. and Bourne, H. (2017) "Managing Dual Identities in Nonprofit Rebranding: An Exploratory Study", *Nonprofit and Voluntary Sector Quarterly* 46 (4), 794–816.

Lucas, E. (2017) "Reinventing the Rattling Tin: How UK Charities Use Facebook in Fundraising", *International Journal of Nonprofit and Voluntary Sector Marketing* 22 (2), e1576.

MacQuillin, I., Sargeant, A. and Shang, J. (2016) *Relationship Fundraising: It's Time to Rethink How You Relate to Your Donors,* Plymouth: Pursuant Intelligent Fundraising. Accessed on 21 November 2017 at www.pursuant.com.

Mato-Santiso, V., Rey-García, M. and Sanzo-Pérez, M. (2021) "Managing Multi-Stakeholder Relationships in Nonprofit organizations Through Multiple Channels: A Systematic Review and Research Agenda for Enhancing Stakeholder Relationship Marketing", *Public Relations Review* 47 (4), 102074.

McAllister, S. (2013) "Toward a Dialogic Theory of Fundraising", *Community College Journal of Research and Practice* 37 (4), 262–277.

Michaelidou, N., Micevski, M. and Cadogan, J. (2015) "An Evaluation of Nonprofit Brand Image: Toward a Better Conceptualisation and Measurement", *Journal of Business Research* 68 (8), 1657–1666.

Michel, G. and Rieunier, S. (2012) "Nonprofit Brand Image and Typicality Influences on Charitable Giving", *Journal of Business Research* 65 (5), 701–707.

Ong, J. (2015) "Charity Appeals as 'Pornography Porn'? Production Ethics in Representing Suffering Children and Typhoon Haiyan Beneficiaries in the Philippines". In Banks, M., Conor, B. and Mayer. V. (Eds), *Production Studies, the Sequel! Cultural Studies of Global Media Industries,* 1–27, New York: Routledge.

Sargeant, A., Ford, J. and Hudson, J. (2008) "Charity Brand Personality: The Relationship with Giving Behaviour", *Nonprofit and Voluntary Sector Quarterly* 37 (3), 468–491.

Sargeant, A. and Hudson, J. (2007) "Donor Retention: An Exploratory Study of Door-to-Door Recruits", *International Journal of Nonprofit and Voluntary Sector Marketing* 13 (1), 89–101.

Sauve-Rodd, J. (2007) "Donor Profitability Measurement", *Journal of Direct, Data and Digital Marketing Practice* 9 (1), 47–66.

Smitko, K. (2012) "Donor Engagement Through Twitter", *Public Relations Review* 36 (4), 633–635.

Stride, H. (2006) "An Investigation of the Values Dimension of Branding: Implications for the Charity Sector", *International Journal of Nonprofit and Voluntary Sector Marketing* 11 (2), 115–124.

Tapp, A. (1996) "Charity Brands: A Qualitative Study of Current Practice", *International Journal of Nonprofit and Voluntary Sector Marketing* 1 (4), 327–336.

Voeth, M. and Herbst, U. (2008) "The Concept of Brand Personality as an Instrument for Advanced Nonprofit Branding: An Empirical Analysis", *Journal of Nonprofit and Voluntary Sector Marketing* 19 (1), 71–97.

Waters, R. (2009) "The Importance of Understanding Donor Preferences and Relationship Cultivation Strategies", *Journal of Nonprofit and Public Sector Marketing* 21 (4), 327–346.

Wymer, W. and Gross, H. (2021) "Charity Advertising: A Literature Review and Research Agenda", *Journal of Philanthropy and Marketing* Early View, e1723.

Xu, J. (2022) "The Impact of Guilt and Shame in Charity Advertising: The Role of Self-Construal", *Journal of Philanthropy and Marketing* 27 (1), e1709.

Xu, J. and Huang, G. (2020) "The Relative Effectiveness of Gain-Framed and Loss-Framed Messages in Charity Advertising: Meta-Analytic Evidence and Implications", *International Journal of Nonprofit and Voluntary Sector Marketing* 25 (4), e1675.

4　Fundraising today and tomorrow

This chapter covers research relating to developments in the fundraising field that have arisen consequent to the public's increasing use of the Internet to make charitable donations. Additionally, it deals with research concerning the Internet-related issues of (i) the employment of social media by nonprofit organisations to promote causes and to secure donations, (ii) content marketing, (iii) the rise of fundraising through mobile devices (especially smartphones), and (iv) fundraising via crowdfunding and telethons. The chapter concludes with discussions of research into fundraising via sports events and into the acquisition of major gifts (including legacies).

Online giving is direct, convenient for donors, and is today routinely practiced by people of all ages. A major advantage to nonprofits of online giving is that organisations can respond immediately and inexpensively to donors online and, importantly, they can incorporate into messages videos that show a nonprofit's beneficiaries. Social media (i.e., websites and platforms that enable people to create and share communications with others and to participate in online social networking) have become an integral and important part of the contemporary nonprofit fundraising scene. If donations occur through social networking platforms (i.e., technologies that make possible the deployment of social media services – Facebook or Twitter for example), donors can subsequently interact, and hence bond, with a nonprofit. Also, donors can incorporate other supporters of a nonprofit into their social networks, may share content about the relevant cause, and might experience a sense of community through being among people who share their interest in the same cause. Nevertheless, online fundraising is not without problems. Zheng, Niu, and Wang (2023), for instance, observed how website browsers commonly avoided online charity fundraising information. The authors completed two studies (involving 274 and 290 participants, respectively) using data obtained from a professional online survey platform. Outcomes from both the investigations suggested that 'browsing intention' in relation to charities was influenced by the emotionality of the fundraising organisation's donation page title, a person's perceptions of the charity's credibility, levels of cognitive and emotional empathy, and the individual's donation history.

DOI: 10.4324/9781003364405-4

Increasingly, giving occurs through mobile devices: usually smartphones. Donating via a mobile device offers the giver total flexibility over the timing of gifts and hence is ideal for one-off impulse donations, e.g., following an appeal broadcast on television or during a 'telethon'. Donors frequently use texts from mobile devices to make small gifts to television-based fundraising events and ad hoc appeals. Texting is a fast and convenient way to give, and one that requires little cognitive effort on the part of the donor. An advantage to the nonprofit is that the fundraiser obtains the donor's telephone number. Thus, follow-up communications designed to establish a long-term relationship with the donor can ensue.

Theoretical approaches

A plethora of issues surround online, mobile, and social media fundraising, and the landscape in the area can change so rapidly that it becomes difficult to apply or develop overarching theories capable of explaining activities within the domain. A commendable attempt to do this is contained in Sisson's (2017) investigation of the views of donors regarding the employment of social media platforms by five animal welfare charities. The author applied 'Control Mutuality Theory' to analyse the opinions of 1032 of the sample charities' supporters relating to this matter. Sisson (2017) defined control mutuality as 'the extent to which relational partners agree on who has the right to determine relationship goals' (p. 180). Within a relationship, one of the partners may dominate, or equal participation in decision-making could apply. Equal participation was preferable, Sisson (2017) argued, because it led to stability in a relationship. Sisson (2017) cited a paper by Sargeant and Lee (2004) to suggest that mutual control would be present when donors felt that, while their views had been influenced or shaped by a nonprofit, they as donors could influence the organisation's policies. Control mutuality required dialogue and feedback from both sides, plus multiple communication flows, and wide stakeholder participation. Sisson's (2017) empirical study surveyed 1,076 supporters of the five animal charities to determine (i) the degrees to which they believed that a nonprofit's social media caused them to feel that they had control mutuality in their relationships with the charities they supported, (ii) the extents to which they engaged with a charity through social media, and (iii) the consequences of social media-induced engagement for relationships. It emerged that donors who 'liked' or followed a charity's social media platforms perceived the presence of greater control mutuality and were more likely to engage in dialogue. Donors who perceived high control mutuality felt that their opinions were valued and that expressions of their opinions influenced the charity.

Another theoretically based study that applied social media related to fundraising issues was Curtis et al.'s (2010) use of the 'Unified Theory of Acceptance and Use of Technology' (UTAUT) to investigate the adoption of social media by nonprofit organisations. The UTAUT Scale has seven dimensions, i.e., performance expectancy, effort expectancy, social influence, facilitating conditions, voluntariness of use, self-efficacy, and anxiety. Curtis et al. (2010) administered the UTAUT Scale to a sample of 409 nonprofit public relations practitioners, finding that social media were seen as a credible means for fundraising (and also for general marketing) and that opinions of social media were favourable. Female participants reported that they found social media to be more useful for fundraising than was reported by males. However, males were more confident than females about the use of social media. An interesting theory-based investigation of the use of social media by a single nonprofit organisation was that of Wilks (2016) who employed Signal Transmission Theory to try to explain how an arts nonprofit communicated its professed values to its stakeholders. Wilks (2016) first analysed the nonprofit's webpages, then its tweets (through the Tweet Archivist Service), and then the communications the organisation had transmitted through Facebook, Instagram, YouTube, Tumblr, and other social media platforms. This identified 15 values that the organisation was attempting to transmit. Next, to examine how the organisation's donors received and decoded the transmitted messages a questionnaire containing a list of the 15 values was distributed online to 108 of the nonprofit's supporters, asking them whether they agree or disagreed with each of the 15 values. Findings from the study indicated that the participants had successfully decoded the messages about the organisation's values sent to them via social media channels. Facebook was especially important as a means of communication.

The transmission of electronic word-of-mouth (eWoM) is a major concern of fundraisers operating in online environments. EWoM involves statements made available to a large audience through social media and is important because eWoM messages remain until they are deleted (in contrast to conventional word-of-mouth where comments disappear as soon as they are spoken). A study completed by Pressgrove, McKeever, and Jang (2018) employed the STEPPS model to evaluate message factors that might affect eWoM in a nonprofit context. STEPPS stands for 'social currency' (i.e., the desire to look good in front of others), 'triggers' (motivations to act), 'emotion', 'practical value' (usefulness), 'public' (being highly visible), and 'stories' (to educate and entertain). The authors completed a content analysis of 1,000 tweets arising from the 'Ice Bucket Challenge' charity fundraising organisation. The themes most prevalent in the tweets were social currency, triggers, and high-arousal emotion. The authors concluded that the STEPPS model provided a credible tool for theory building in the social marketing domain.

Ad hoc studies

Early investigations often explored the extents and natures of nonprofits' uses of social media. Waters, Burnett, Lamm, and Lucas (2009), for instance, analysed the Facebook profiles of 275 nonprofit organisations concluding that, while most of the nonprofits in the sample used Facebook to describe their organisations and to list the names of senior managers, the organisations did not employ Facebook interactively or to broadcast news about campaigns. Moreover, at the time, Facebook had not been incorporated into wider communication strategies. 'Disclosure' and 'transparency seemed to be the major aim of the Facebook activities of the sample organisations. A similar study by Lovejoy and Saxton (2012) investigated how the UK's 100 largest charities utilised Twitter. This study revealed, via a content analysis of the tweets of the 100 organisations, that Twitter was being used strategically and comprehensively. As well as employing Twitter to provide factual information, the medium had been employed to thank donors for their support and to respond to messages. Also, the charities were using Twitter to promote events, to appeal directly for donations, and to sell merchandise. The authors attributed the sudden rise in interest in Twitter among nonprofits to the organisations in question having quickly acquired the know-how necessary to make effective use of social media. Previously their fundraising managers did not possess this knowledge. Compared to general online fundraising, Twitter was easy to

---

Box 4.1 Research opportunities: social media platforms

Clearly, platform effectiveness is an under-researched subject that is worthy of considerable further investigation. At present, research findings in the area are incomplete and incapable of generalisation. Thus, future research in the field needs to be wide-ranging and to abstract from individual nonprofit organisations' circumstances. For instance, few studies have examined the degrees to which nonprofits apply a strategic focus when managing social media. What factors influence the adoption of strategic approaches; what are the consequences of strategic approaches and what are the barriers to their successful adoption? As regards particular platforms, what are the likely future trajectories of Twitter, Facebook, etc., and how will changes in direction impact on opportunities for fundraising? Many studies of the uses of Twitter, Instagram, etc., by nonprofits have found that the platforms have been employed predominantly for information dissemination, and that their application has often been occasional and reactive. If this is true, then why is it the case? Can a comprehensive and integrated model of the intensity of use of Twitter, etc., be constructed and statistically estimated to predict fundraising outcomes? What sorts of organisational arrangement are associated with effective social media management?

use (as was Facebook), had built-in interactivity, and offered a wide range of user metrics. Hence it was easier for nonprofits to engage strategically with stakeholders than was the case using ordinary websites. Conversely, a US study of 73 nonprofits undertaken by Lovejoy, Waters and Saxton (2012) concluded that the sample organisations were using Twitter primarily for one-way communication, and not for stimulating stakeholder involvement. The authors examined the tweet frequency, use of hyperlinks, hashtags, retweets and 'following behaviour' of the 73 nonprofits, finding few 'conversations'. The organisations were not making the most of the new possibilities for connecting with stakeholders that Twitter offered.

Social media and donation behaviour

Several studies have explored the impact on donor behaviour of fundraisers' use of social media. Saxton and Wang (2014), for instance, identified significant 'Social Network Effects' that influenced giving through social media. Social network effects occur in situations where people create, share and exchange information and ideas within virtual communities. The authors analysed the genres of fundraising message placed on the 'Facebook Causes' platform by 66 large US nonprofits, plus the numbers of donors to the 66 nonprofits and the timings of and amounts given to the nonprofits by individuals via the Facebook Causes platform. They also obtained data from the US Inland Revenue Service on the total revenues raised by the same organisations. It emerged that messages designed to arouse attention, to relate to social pressures, and to stimulate impulse donations were more effective for raising money than messages that contained 'rational' messages describing a nonprofit's efficiency. Social network effects significantly explained total online donations. It seemed that information about the charities had indeed been spread by donors who had donated via the Facebook Causes platform, and this may have impelled other people to donate. Also, compared to people who donated offline, online donors tended to give to different types of nonprofits, especially to health-related causes. The term 'social media traction' refers to measures for improving an organisation's web platform ranking in order to attract more browsers to the organisation's website. Shin (2019) investigated the impact of social media on the performance of nonprofit organisations via an analysis of 100 nonprofit fundraising organisations ranked by web traction measures, including Facebook Likes and Twitter Followers. The results indicated that nonprofits with higher web traction had substantially more donations and grants than organisations with lower web traction. The authors suggested that the use of social media promoted better interactive (two-way) communications with the public, leading to the attraction of more supporters and increased charitable giving. However, the findings also showed that the impacts of (i) general economic conditions, and (ii) a charity's non-web based fundraising activities, had greater influences on charitable giving than the impact of web traction.

Another notable contribution in the online donor behaviour area was an investigation by Wallace, Buil and de Chernatony (2017) of the influence of 'conspicuous' online giving (defined as the situation where individuals mention on a social media platform the fact that they have donated to a particular nonprofit) on the offline donations of a sample of young people. The authors surveyed 234 young donors about the matter, finding that individuals who mentioned charities online were significantly likely to give higher amounts offline. The authors attributed this outcome to the possibility that conspicuous donating online enabled individuals to state something about their true selves, and that this affected their offline giving behaviour. As part of their study, Wallace, Buil, and de Chernatony (2017) explored the effects on conspicuous donating behaviour of the sample members' personal traits of self-esteem, materialism, and self-monitoring (i.e., sensitivity to surrounding cues and hence consistency of self-presentation in any situation). Materialistic people were more likely than others to engage in both self- and other-orientated conspicuous donating.

Facebook has figured prominently in research investigating the influence of social media on giving behaviour. A study that examined directly the effects of donor interactions with Facebook on giving behaviour was that of Algharat et al. (2018), which hypothesised that interactions between potential donors and a nonprofit organisation's page on Facebook would result in the potential donors (i) using their imaginations about and socially interacting with the organisation, (ii) experiencing feelings of human warmth and sociability, and (iii) wanting to *engage* with the nonprofit's Facebook page. Additionally, the authors posited that donor engagement that had been induced by social media would lead to increased eWoM and willingness to donate to a nonprofit. The mechanisms whereby this would occur, Algharat et al. (2018) suggested, involved 'telepresence' (i.e., the sense of being present within a computer-mediated environment); involvement (defined for the purpose of the study as internal arousal); and 'social presence'. The last of these, social presence, related to social media's capacity to enable potential donors to engage psychologically with other people who were interested in a particular nonprofit and to perceive themselves as psychologically close to these people. A survey of 400 (non-student) Facebook fans of nonprofit organisations in Jordan indicated that telepresence, social presence and involvement significantly determined engagement, which in turn significantly influenced eWoM and willingness to donate. Xue and Zhou (2022) examined the effects of different types of Facebook fundraising posts on donor engagement. Several types of possible social influence were investigated: strength of relationship with the fundraiser, urgency of the fundraising need, and number of donations shown on a page. An online experiment was completed with 357 participants (aged between 18 and 77) using perceived source credibility, feeling of social presence, attitude toward the post, and intention to click, share, and donate as the dependent variables. It emerged that Facebook fundraising posts for an 'urgent' need generated many more positive responses than posts for a nonurgent need.

As regards Instagram, Mendini, Peter and Maione (2022) completed two laboratory experimental studies using 291 and 234 student participants, respectively, to explore the effects of time spent on Instagram on feelings of gratitude, altruism, and willingness to donate to charities. The results indicated that time spent on Instagram could have an instant positive effect on individuals. On average, heavy Instagram users expressed more gratitude, felt more altruistic, and donated more than light users.

Content marketing

Content marketing concerns the creation and broadcast of useful information and comment via webpages, blogs, e-newsletters, videos, podcasts, apps, tweets, Facebook communications, and so on. Many nonprofits have invested heavily in content marketing, and a large number of consultancy businesses specialising in content marketing now serve their (still growing) needs. The influence of consultants on nonprofits' content marketing activities was examined in a paper by Bennett (2017), who compared the views and opinions of content marketing held by (i) 239 fundraising managers, (ii) 489 donors to UK charities, and (iii) 105 heads of consultancy businesses that offered nonprofit content marketing services. Participants in the study were asked about their perceptions of the importance of four supposed objectives of content marketing; namely search engine optimisation (i.e., the pursuit of high search page rankings), 'impression management' (i.e., attempts at engendering good impressions of a nonprofit among potential donors), creating transparency vis-à-vis a nonprofit's operations, and transmitting messages that 'go viral'. Several differences of opinion emerged among the three groups. For example, fundraising managers believed that donors were impressed by high search page rankings, but donors themselves tended not to hold this view. Fundraisers and their consultants thought it was appropriate for a nonprofit to avoid publicly discussing its difficulties, whereas donors believed that charities should disclose problematic issues. At the same time, while fundraisers felt it necessary for nonprofits to supply detailed information about their organisations' structures and finances, donors and consultants generally thought that such disclosures were not required. The last of these outcomes (that donors were unimpressed by the provision of information on organisation structures and finances), was comparable to the results of studies completed by Szper and Prakash (2011) and by Leventhal and Foot (2015). Szper and Prakash (2011) found that information disclosures among a sample of 90 US nonprofits in Washington did not increase donations. The authors concluded that this was because the effects of information disclosure were intertwined with a donor's familiarity with a nonprofit, with word-of-mouth, and with the nonprofit's visibility in the community. Leventhal and Foot's (2015) examination of possible connections between (i) the 'performance and financial signals' disclosed by Australian nonprofit organisations, and (ii) household giving to these organisations, failed to reveal any significant relationships. An

---

Box 4.2   Research opportunities: online donor behaviour and content marketing

An important issue for future research is how content marketing can best be employed in nonprofit branding. It has been suggested that because many people are short of time, they desire communications that are short and to the point. If so, then research should explore how nonprofits' social media campaigns can fit into lifestyles that involve perceptions of time shortage. It is relevant to note that the average consumer in Western Europe and North America is now connected through several different addressable devices (on average five per person in the UK). Further research opportunities arise vis-à-vis the measurement of the effectiveness of nonprofits' 'native' fundraising advertisements, i.e., advertisements integrated into social media communications? For instance, how can nonprofits devise successful native advertising strategies? How is native advertising best included in mobile communications?

Smartphone applications are being used for a rapidly increasing number of daily-life activities, and a number of fundraising nonprofits have adapted or are in the process of adapting their materials (videos, livestreaming devices [i.e., visual storytelling], etc.) and the messages employed in appeals to make them suitable for smartphone viewing. Research is needed into how the personalisation of touch points between a nonprofit and a donor should proceed in a world where the donor's main mode of communication is through a smartphone. A significant problem reported in the grey literature on fundraising concerns the difficulty of breaking into the 'filter bubbles' that allegedly surround certain users of social media. Filter bubbles result from 'algorithmic bias', i.e., the capacity of heavy social media use to limit people's social experience thus trapping them in 'echo chambers' of opinion wherein their existing views are reinforced and amplified. Allegedly, it can be hard for fundraisers to break through a filter and hence create an emotional connection with a potential donor who mentally resides within a bubble. Research might seek to establish the causes and effects of algorithmic bias.

experiment conducted by Xiao, Huang, Bortree, and Waters (2022) examined the effects of fundraising message content characteristics on donation intentions through a simulated social media campaign. A two (abstract versus concrete message) × two (gain vs. loss framing) experimental design was applied to a sample of 213 participants using a real childhood cancer charity: World Child Cancer. (A gain-framed message emphasises the potential benefits of acting upon an appeal, whereas a loss-framed message highlights the negative consequences of noncompliance.) The findings of this particular study suggested that a message which contained detailed information on fundraising outcomes elicited greater intentions to donate. This was because the provision of details on outcomes increased the sample members' perceptions of message credibility and transparency, and was associated with cognitive elaboration and the arousal of empathy. However, gain and loss framing did not result in significant differences in donation intentions.

Crowdfunding

Online communication with potential donors has facilitated the use of 'crowdfunding' by nonprofits to finance specific projects. Crowdfunding occurs when a nonprofit obtains funds from a large audience (the 'crowd') via the Internet and where each member of the crowd contributes a relatively small amount of money. The method alters not only the way in which a nonprofit can finance new capital investments, but also the manner whereby people can give, i.e., a donor can choose the *specific* projects the individual wishes to support and may thereby express a particular self-identity when making a donation. Also, the donor can engage with other donors through social media, exchanging stories, and perhaps narrating personal experiences involving the supported project. Donors are able to chat about a project and may communicate the crowdfunded campaign to friends, relatives, and work colleagues. Giving becomes less private and outcomes more transparent.

The social media aspect of crowdfunding was explored in a study by Stiver, Barroca, and Minocha (2015) who observed how donors could forge bonds with other supporters of the same project, creating thereby 'collective motives' to give. The authors posed the question 'what is the balance between individual motives and collective motives when a person donates to a crowdfunded project'? Fan-Osuala, Zantedeschi, and Jank (2017) commented on the rapid growth in the number of platforms supporting crowdfunding that had occurred in the decade preceding their study. The authors' review of past literature on the topic reported findings from studies which had examined crowdfunding campaign duration, type of cause, the effects of using celebrity endorsers, 'quality signals' and their effects on public perceptions of the feasibility of a project, and target amount to be raised. Their own investigation compared successful and unsuccessful campaigns in order to construct an econometric model capable of predicting outcomes to crowdfunding campaigns. Another survey of the extant crowdfunding literature (plus an analysis of 250 Italian social enterprise crowdfunding campaigns) completed by Balboni and Kocollari (2017) concluded that choice of platform, campaign design, the size of a nonprofit's network, and the careful use of Twitter constituted the main factors associated with crowdfunding success.

'Success factors' connected with crowdfunding campaigns were also investigated by Liu, Suh, and Wagner (2017), who found that positive outcomes were associated with a nonprofit's ability to stimulate potential donors' empathy with a project, the quality of the nonprofit's website, the reputation of the organisation, and public perceptions of the 'credibility' of a proposed project. The authors developed a stimulus (project characteristics), organism (perceptions of a project's credibility), and response (intention to donate) model of crowd giving. Findings from a sample of 205 people indicated that that website quality, transaction convenience, and project content quality influenced both empathy and perceived credibility, which in turn constituted key determinants of donation intention. Similar results emerged from a study of 206 social media users in China conducted by Li, Hou, Guan, and Chong (2022). In this study, empathy was affected by a donor's perceived proximity to the beneficiary of an appeal and by social influence exerted on social media platforms. High empathy was associated with personal impulsiveness, which also had an impact on donation intention. Social influence involved an individual's perceptions of what other people expected the individual to do, and the desire to maintain satisfying relationships. Another stimulus-organism-response model was employed by Chen, Dai, Wang et al. (2021) to examine the factors that encouraged a sample of 436 Chinese crowdfunding donors to experience positive donation intentions. Outcomes indicated that perceived ease of use, perceived self-efficacy, and social connection with a beneficiary had significant effects on giving intentions.

The effectiveness of various types of content of crowdfunding appeals has been the subject of attention. For instance, a study by Buskila and Perez (2022) of 200 projects funded by 5,031 donors that were launched on a major online global charity crowdfunding platform between December 2018 and December 2019 concluded that, other things being equal, campaign photographs which portrayed victims who did not seem to be engaged in any form of self-help elicited lower donations compared with pictures that displayed beneficiaries who were taking action to address their circumstances. According to a study completed by Ge, Zhang and Zhao (2022), different types of negative emotions (sadness, anxiety, and fear) expressed in crowdfunding project descriptions affect donations. The authors collected data on 15,653 projects across four categories (medical, educational, disaster, and poverty assistance) from an online crowdfunding platform in China presented between September 2013 and May 2019. In the medical assistance category, expressions of sadness exerted an inverted U-shaped effect on donations, while the expression of anxiety had a negative effect. In the education and disaster relief categories, expressions of sadness had positive influences on donations, whereas anxiety and fear had no impact. Expressions of sadness, anxiety, and fear had no influence on donations in the poverty assistance category. Such findings are interesting and, if they are generalisable internationally, they have crucial implications for the design of crowdfunding campaigns. Further research is needed to replicate this study, perhaps including additional mediating and moderating variables, in order to confirm or question the findings. This applies also to another study that assessed connections between text and pictures in crowdfunding appeals that was completed by Lee and Park (2020), who collected textual and visual contents from a large South Korean online donation crowdfunding platform. Six hundred and sixty-three projects created by 317 organisations were examined in terms of visual (image) and textural (text) contents of the project, target amount, duration, and current donation amount and current number of donors. It emerged that the observation of a physically small recipient within images led to a strong willingness to help, that the expression of positive emotions in an appeal could depress potential donors' empathy toward the recipient (because positive emotions could seem inconsistent with the recipients' situation), and that complex project descriptions required more effort to understand recipients' circumstances, possibly causing potential donors to hesitate. In this study, sad facial images of recipients did not increase potential donors' participation.

It is relevant to consider in this connection the substantial amount of research that has been undertaken into the roles of facial expressions in fundraising contexts other than crowdfunding. For instance, the results from three studies (involving 100, 160, and 100 adults, respectively) completed by Jang (2022) indicated that happy facial expressions and 'cuteness' influenced both empathy and donations. Happy expressions led to greater perceived cuteness, which in turn generated empathy and charitable gifts. Pham and Septianto (2019) concluded from experiments conducted on 212 participants that people allocated a higher donation amount to a charity when they saw an image of a sad-faced child combined with a request message (e.g., 'please donate'), or an image of a happy-faced child combined with a 'recognition message' such as 'thank you'. A survey undertaken in China by Li and Yin (2022) found interaction effects between facial expressions, the number of beneficiaries shown in an advertisement, and donation intentions. An advertisement that included a single sad-faced beneficiary attracted greater donation intentions than an advertisement which displayed multiple sad-faced beneficiaries. Conversely, an advertisement containing multiple happy-faced beneficiaries was more effective than an advertisement displaying a single beneficiary.

Theories proffered as possible explanations of the attractiveness of crowdfunding include the Theory of Affordances (suggested by Choy and Schlagwein, 2017), and Self-System Theory as espoused by Zong and Lin (2017).

'Affordances' are properties of an artefact that determine how it is perceived and its possible uses, e.g., a chair will be perceived as enabling a person to sit down. Choy and Schlagwein (2017) examined the relationship between information technology affordances and donor motivations to participate in crowdfunding. The authors completed case studies of two charities, observing how IT affordances (e.g., pushing a certain button to afford the downloading of information) could play a crucial role in achieving crowdfunding success. They concluded that social media platform affordances stimulated nonprofit donations in ways not found in offline fundraising, and hence that careful interface design was vital. Self-System Theory embraces a collection of factors that describe the self (e.g., self-esteem, self-perception and evaluation, self-efficacy), and which are assumed to explain behaviour. Zong and Lin (2017) applied Self-System Theory to explore, within online environments, donors' motives to give to crowdfunding appeals. The authors identified six clusters of types of people prepared to participate in crowdfunding. The clusters comprised donors who were inert (i.e., occasional), active (i.e., frequent), rational (who often donated but only gave small amounts), bounteous, chaotic (who exhibited no coherent pattern of giving), and masked (who kept their giving secret). Crowdfunding donors typically balanced altruism against self-interest, the authors suggested.

Box 4.3   Research opportunities: crowdfunding

Several promising areas for future research exist in the crowdfunding field. Donor motives for engaging in crowdfunding have received scant attention. How do these motives compare with motives to donate in other ways? How precisely can supporters express their individuality through donating to crowdfunded projects? Often a donor's name will appear on the website of a crowdfunded project. How great an incentive is this to a potential donor? Do shock tactics, guilt appeals, etc., work in the same way for crowdfunding as for other fundraising methods, and if so how and why? Considering that crowdfunding software is inexpensive, can small nonprofits compete effectively with large (sometimes international) nonprofits vis-à-vis crowdfunding, and if so how? How far might a charity's donor base be extended by crowdfunding, and what are the techniques that are the most likely to extend the reach? What factors determine when, how and why donors to a crowdfunded project communicate with each other on social media? What types of new donor might crowdfunding attract?

Disintermediation

Some forms of crowdfunding constitute examples of disintermediation, i.e., situations that occur when a donor gives *directly* to an individual or a cause (for instance via a crowdfunding site) and thus bypasses the charity sector altogether. In the UK, disintermediation has expanded rapidly and extensively, due perhaps to many donors preferring to support visible and 'direct causes' that offer social rewards, e.g., a greater sense of ownership, transparency of the use of a gift, and proximity to the supported person or cause. Also, a donor might not trust charities and/or may perceive charities as incompetent and to spend too much on administration. Kottasz, MacQuillin, and Bennett (2022) outlined a number of problems associated with the practice. For instance, disintermediated giving could lead to an influx of untrained and unknowledgeable fundraisers, i.e., people who lack the skills and management insights to distribute money effectively, who become responsible for managing donations. Disintermediated giving is unregulated and unaccountable in most countries at present, and substantial amounts of money which would otherwise be given to charities are diverted away from orthodox fundraising organisations. No tax relief is available for gifts to beneficiaries not registered as charities.

Wymer and Čačija (2022) identified various responses that conventional charities could make to the 'disintermediation threat', notably the development of an organisation's reputation, strengthening its brand, improving the management of donors' overall giving experience, and pointing out the

---

Box 4.4   Research opportunities: disintermediation

Disintermediation is one of the major new topics in fundraising to have arisen over the last few years. Research in the area needs to include case studies on how conventional charities have responded to the challenge and the success factors involved. Several versions of disintermediation exist, so a robust typology of various options outlining the features, difficulties and risks associated with each form would be useful. To what extent do members of the public recognise the opportunities for fraud arising from unregulated disintermediated giving? What factors determine an individual donor's awareness of risks of fraud relating to disintermediation and what sort of conceptual model might explain public perceptions? What determines a potential donor's level of sensitivity to disintermediation scandals? From the viewpoint of the beneficiary, what communication and other promotional methods are most effective for raising funds? Why have government and regulatory bodies not intervened in the control and supervision of disintermediated giving projects? What sorts of regulatory control would be most appropriate? Disintermediation is probably here to stay, so how is the practice likely to develop and to what degree is it likely to cannibalise the revenues of orthodox fundraising charities? The rise of disintermediated giving has offered donors a wider choice of giving opportunities than hitherto, but might this lead to 'donor fatigue' and eventual disinterest in the method? At the theoretical level it could be worthwhile to compare and contrast disintermediation with experiences of 'disruptive technologies' in the commercial sector.

More research on the framing of disintermediation appeals is required. What visual imagery works best for disintermediated campaigns? What emotional responses need to be invoked by an appeal? Additional areas for investigation include analyses of differences in demographics between charity donors and disintermediated donors; the sorts of heuristics applied; how word-of-mouth referrals operate in disintermediation settings, and details of the disintermediated 'donor journey'. What aspects of individual beneficiaries make them especially attractive? What sorts of story narrative are most likely to appeal to potential donors?

risks associated with fraudulent disintermediated appeals. Charities could, moreover, provide more customised fundraising campaigns for specific projects or individuals in need. The framing of effective disintermediated appeals is clearly worthy of investigation, but to date little research has addressed this matter. One study that has explored the topic was undertaken by Sepehri et al. (2021) who, through four field and laboratory studies, found that direct appeal narratives written in the first person by an intended recipient were likely to raise less money than narratives written in the third person by a third party on behalf of the intended recipient. Prospective donors appeared to ascribe less credibility to direct appeals, and this curtailed their willingness to give.

Telethons

Another fundraising medium that has been greatly facilitated by the availability of online giving (especially through the use of smartphones) is the telethon, i.e., a television programme, typically presented in an emotionally charged manner and sometimes lasting for several hours, that is designed to raise funds for a single or a selection of causes. Viewers watch celebrity performers who support a particular good cause, comedy sketches of people performing hilarious stunts, and constant appeals for donations. The aim of the content of a telethon is to create a sense of involvement with the cause(s) shown during the broadcast. Often, telethons feature third world poverty and problems found mainly in economically underdeveloped countries.

Research into the fundraising effectiveness of telethons has been limited, and the studies that have been completed have been somewhat critical of the contents of the telethons they examined. An early study of a single cause telethon (featuring muscular dystrophy) was undertaken by Feldman and Feldman (1985) who questioned 60 undergraduate students both before and after viewing the telethon about their attitudes towards (i) disabled people and (ii) their financial donation behaviour regarding disability issues. Watching the telethon exerted an immediate, positive and long-term impact on the students' attitudes, but had no effect on actual donations when compared with the giving behaviour of a non-viewing control group. This result, Feldman and Feldman (1985) concluded, challenged the value of telethons for raising funds. Later studies have tended to focus on the negative images of beneficiaries that are frequently displayed during telethons. Jefferess (2002), for example, argued that telethons routinely depicted images of third world poverty and not of the transformational developments currently occurring in third world countries. 'The image of the emaciated or malnourished, dirty, desperate-looking child has become critical to telethon fundraising' Jefferess (2002) opined, and the projection of such images 'normalise' sights of third world poverty (p. 3). Victims, Jefferess (2002) continued, were shown as being totally dependent on the viewing audience's charitable donations. Scenes were carefully orchestrated to evoke tears, feelings of guilt within and donations from people in financially better-off nations. Portrayals of the disabled have been the subject of particular opprobrium in the research literature on telethons. A study of a disability telethon undertaken by Longmore (2005) noted how 'being looked at is one of the social experiences of being disabled' and that disability telethons involved 'mass staring' at disabled people (p. 503). Staring, according to Longmore (2005) enacts a form of relationship that constitutes the people doing the staring as being normal and the object of the stares as being different.

Bhati and McDonnell (2020) examined attempts by fundraising organisations to utilise social media to support fundraising activities associated with an online 'Giving Day'. The authors tested several hypotheses relating to the effectiveness of employing Facebook for fundraising purposes by 704 nonprofits that participated in a US telethon entitled 'Omaha Gives'. Findings suggested that fundraising success (measured in terms of number of donors and value of donations) was positively and significantly associated with a nonprofit organisation's Facebook network size (defined as number of likes), activity (number of posts), and audience engagement (number of shares with other people). Organisational factors such as budget size, age of the nonprofit, and the cause addressed by an organisation's programmes also exerted significant influences.

Disaster relief fundraising

Telethons are sometimes used (in conjunction with newspaper advertising) to help disaster relief charities to raise funds following major environmental catastrophes (floods, earthquakes, tsunamis, etc.). Only a limited amount of academic research has assessed the effectiveness of emergency fundraising for disaster relief. An early paper by Bennett and Kottasz (2000) questioned 200 members of the general public in central London to ascertain the factors that encouraged them to give to disaster relief appeals. It emerged that highly emotive images of the indigence of victims were best for evoking donations, even though the portrayals might be deemed demeaning to the victims involved. Scenes of local people helping themselves were also useful for stimulating donations. Negative influences on giving included media reports of unfair aid distributions, of inefficient relief operations, and of the presence of warfare in an area. Combined appeals by several charities acting together (as happens in the UK through the Disasters Emergency Committee [www. dec.org.uk]) raised more money in total than the sum of specific charities making individual appeals.

Waters (2013) sought to answer the intriguing question of whether extensive media coverage of a natural disaster stimulates donations to the relief organisations operating in the location of the disaster. The author analysed the television coverage of three natural disasters that had been broadcast within the six weeks following each of the natural disasters, and the extents of the television coverage of five major nonprofits that had provided relief following each disaster. The information obtained from the analysis was then compared with fundraising data from the five nonprofits. The authors concluded that widespread coverage did not normally lead to increased donations; an outcome which the authors noted was similar to those of previous investigations. However, donation levels 'spiked' for particular nonprofits on the days when they were mentioned in newscasts. A different outcome regarding this matter was obtained by Chapman, Hornsey, Fielding, and Gulliver (2022), whose survey of 949 Australians found that donors' perceptions of the magnitudes of news coverage of an event constituted a strong influence on the amount they donated to bushfire disaster appeals. Moreover, media coverage was a more influential determinant of participants' charity selection than either peer influence or direct communications from charities.

A limited amount of research has been completed in relation to the contents of disaster relief appeals. Zhou and Xue (2019) examined the effects of (i) colour format (i.e., text only, text with black-and-white photo, text with full-coloured photo, or text with colour highlighted on the main visual subject), and (ii) issue involvement (high versus low) on the psychological reactions to disaster relief advertisements (attitude, feeling of empathy, and intention to help) of samples of US students and members of the general public. Results from both sets of participants suggested that advertisements

---

Box 4.5   Research opportunities: disaster relief fundraising

Compared to other areas, disaster relief fundraising has been the subject of relatively little empirical research. Several aspects of the subject merit attention. Each disaster is unique in some way. To what extent are common fundraising appeal messages effective when used to raise money for different kinds of disaster? Is a short-term disaster relief appeal likely to cannibalise donations to other charitable causes and if so how might cannibalisation be avoided? Often coping with the aftermath of a disaster takes a long time, sometimes several years. How can repeat donations be encouraged to help with long-term relief? How can short-term appeals persuade donors to give to charities that provide longer term humanitarian aid? Much has been written about the expression of 'white saviourism' (i.e., the depiction of white people as liberating, rescuing or uplifting local non-white victims) explicit in many disaster relief appeals. Frequently this relates to portrayals of the 'vulnerability' of victims. Mezinska et al. (2016) questioned the meaning of 'vulnerability' in the context of disaster relief, noting that the construct is multi-faceted in nature and that donors' perceptions of the nature and degree of local people's vulnerability in a disaster zone can affect donors' willingness to give. Considerably more research into this matter is required.

---

containing photographs (especially black-and-white photographs) created greater positive attitude, empathy, and stronger intention to donate. The effects of the ethnicity of models featured in disaster relief advertisements were investigated by De Pelsmacker, Dens, and De Meulenaer (2022) on a sample of 201 French people and on a separate sample of 194 Indian individuals. Each group was exposed to advertisements that contained Caucasian or Indian models for either a local or a global charity. Findings indicated that the inclusion of models of the same ethnicity as a message recipient resulted in more positive responses for a local charity, while the use of models of a different ethnicity led to more positive responses for a global charity. These effects were mediated by the participants' perceptions of a model's trustworthiness and by their levels of scepticism towards advertising.

The Covid pandemic

The Covid pandemic was of course a major worldwide disaster which had many implications for charity fundraising. Events (marathons, dinners, auctions, golf tournaments, etc.) were cancelled, demands placed on healthcare charities increased, and street collections ceased. At the same time, online fundraising became much more important, e.g., via televised charity fundraising galas. Jin and Ryu (2022) examined within a sample of 1,219 people the psychosocial impact of Covid-related 'mortality salience' (i.e., the strength of a person's awareness of the inevitability of death) on altruism. They concluded that death anxiety and fear significantly predicted feelings of powerlessness and materialism which, in turn, influenced charitable donations. The authors induced awareness of Covid-related mortality within a sub-set of the participants, finding that in this group, people who were the greedier, more selfish, narcissistic, and/or materialistic, made higher monetary donations to charity. Further research is needed into the applicability of Jin and Ryu's (2022) results to other aspects of disaster relief fundraising.

Van Esch, Cui, and Jain (2021) investigated the effects of a donor's self-construal (i.e., a specific belief about the self) and the way in which a persuasive message was framed on donation intent (emphasising either the provision of statistical information or focusing on specific Covid victims). Their research covered 1,104 participants and found that emphasis on identifiable victims had a greater effect on donation intent than statistical information, but only for individuals who possessed an interdependent self-construal, i.e., people who recognised their embeddedness in a network of social relationships and who downplayed their own 'separateness' and unique traits. The authors attributed this result to the heightened holistic thinking style characteristic of interdependent people. Organisational responses to the pandemic were explored by Herrero and Kraemer (2022) who interviewed 91 nonprofit fundraisers during the pandemic's early stages. Interviews queried how the respondents' charities had devised alternative ways of fundraising in order to compensate for the drop in revenues that the pandemic entailed. On average the organisations had increased their use of social media from 12% before the pandemic to 25% during the pandemic. However, digital activities had sometimes been unsuccessful due to lack of digital fundraising skills within charities. Successful organisations demonstrated agility, frequent use of online communication, awareness of the need to employ new technologies, wider participation in social networks (thus providing more information and access to loans and gifts) and the application of fewer targets and plans.

Sporting events

Television-based fundraising can be attached to major charity-related sporting events, e.g., the marathons with 'fun run' participants that take place in major cities. Also, nonprofits sometimes sponsor their own sporting events (running, swimming, obstacle races, etc.) in order to raise funds. Individuals pay an entry fee and, in many cases, supplement the fee with extra donations obtained from friends, family and/or work colleagues. Research in this area has focused on participants' motives for taking part in such events. A summary of these motives was presented in a study undertaken by Won and Park (2010), who concluded that the main motives were philanthropic desires to support a nonprofit's cause; interest in a sport; social interactions with other people; peer group pressures; and wanting to belong to a group. Bennett, Mousley, Kitchin, and Ali-Choudhury (2007) obtained similar results via a survey of 579 participants in nonprofit sponsored sporting events in Greater London. Primary motives for participation were personal involvement with a cause, the opportunity to do something associated with a healthy lifestyle, and the desire to mix socially. Additionally, the authors found that the degree of an individual's 'serious-mindedness' affected the strength of a person's willingness to take part. (A serious-minded person is orientated towards achieving goals seen as important physically or psychologically and thus is likely to take part in a challenging sporting event.) As regards barriers to raising money at sporting events, outcomes to 27 semi-structured interviews undertaken by Filo, Fechner, and Inoue (2020) with participants in a Triathlon identified four major constraints: poor receptivity and lack of funds among potential donors, discomfort in asking for donations, and lack of time.

A further motivating influence was added to the abovementioned lists by Coghlan and Filo (2013) who suggested that feelings of 'connectedness' with other participants, with the nonprofit's cause, and with the self could induce participation. Connectedness related to 'becoming part' of something, sharing beliefs and desires, and self-recognition. To execute the study one of the authors underwent an 'autoethnographic' procedure that included participant observation at a sporting event, recording the author's personal participatory experiences, and critically reflecting on these experiences. Apart from connectedness, the main motivators uncovered by the investigation were a participant's desires for escapism, involvement with a cause, self-esteem, physical enjoyment, and achievement and recognition.

Research to date has not found significant and substantial linkages between taking part in an event and giving to a charity in the longer term. Woolf, Heere, and Walker (2013), for instance, examined this matter via a mixed methods case study of sports events organised by a cancer charity. The authors completed focus groups, interviews with nonprofit managers, participant observation, and a survey of 262 event participants. It emerged that taking part in events did not lead to later relationships with the charity.

Major gift and legacy fundraising

This final section of the present chapter deals with research connected to the important topic of major gift and legacy fundraising. MGF delivers large proportions of the incomes of many nonprofit organisations. Hence, it is vital that fundraisers identify and recruit potential major donors and thereafter build good relationships with them. MGF has received much attention in the practitioner literature, focusing on how best to cultivate prospects, how to craft the solicitation, and the appropriate information to offer a potential major donor about a nonprofit's current and intended projects (see Sargeant, Eisenstein, and Kottasz [2015] for an extensive review of relevant sources within the practitioner literature). However, relatively little academic research has been undertaken into MGF. Noting the absence of theories and models concerning MGF, Knowles and Gomes (2009) proposed the application of an 'AID-TIM' approach to MGF management. The AID-TIM process required (i) the arousal within a prospect of awareness and understanding, interest, and involvement and hence a desire to help, (ii) requesting the prospect to make a 'trial gift', i.e., a small project requiring only a modest level of funding, (iii) providing copious amounts of 'information' about how to give (tax incentives, 'planned giving schemes', etc.), and (iv) obtaining a major gift and implementing 'major gift action' procedures to express appreciation and to build a good relationship with the donor (p. 400). Knowles and Gomes' (2009) research was conceptual in nature and did not test any of these propositions. Mayo (2021) analysed the effects of big gifts made to certain charities on gifts by other donors to rival charities. The author collected information from published sources on 218 large gifts made during the period 1998–2017, finding evidence of the presence of positive spillovers on donations to charities that were 'close' to the recipient of a particular big gift, but negative spillovers on charities that donors viewed as substitutes.

Sargeant et al. (2015) examined the MGF practices and achievements of a sample of 'small' US nonprofits (i.e., with incomes of less than $1 million a year) in order to establish how major gifts were solicited and to determine critical MGF performance success factors. Sargeant et al.'s (2015) investigation concluded that, as well as devoting resources to the acquisition of new major donors, fundraisers needed to concentrate heavily on the retention of existing major donors. Also, fundraisers should segment target donors very precisely, and should engage members of nonprofits' governing boards closely in MGF activities. The nonprofits in Sargeant et al.'s (2015) sample recorded a 32% success rate when soliciting fresh major gift donors and pursued an average of 24 prospects at any one time.

Another study that focused on major gift solicitation was that of Bennett (2012) who questioned the best types of people that a nonprofit should include in an MGF team. One hundred and fifty-one UK charities were surveyed about the matter, the responses suggesting that the most effective MGF team members were individuals who possessed excellent communication and relationship nurturing skills, who already networked among prospective donors, and who were inwardly committed to the MGF function. The need for fundraisers to understand effective techniques for building sound relationships with high-value donors was emphasised in a study undertaken by Drollinger (2017) who recommended the method of 'Active Empathetic Listening' (AEL) as a means for securing major gifts. The steps in AEL were: sensing (to obtain an accurate understanding of a prospect's motives for being prepared to make a large gift), processing the information received, and then responding in suitable manner. AEL required the fundraiser to allow the prospect to dominate conversations and communications and, if it was necessary to ask questions, to make open-ended requests for information.

Legacies

Bequests to charities are a distinctive form of charity giving and represent large proportions of the annual revenues of many fundraising nonprofits; especially larger and better-known organisations. However, academic research in the area has been limited, due perhaps to the sensitivity of the subject and considering that most people dislike being reminded of their own mortality. The effects of potential donors' reluctance to confront mortality were addressed experimentally by Russell and Routley (2016) who presented some, but not all, of their study participants with advertisements that contained stories and appeals for bequests made by *living* individuals. The remaining participants in the study were given advertisements that featured stories and appeals made by *deceased* individuals. All the stories in the advertisements were identical regardless of whether they were communicated by a living person or by a deceased person. The advertisements were distributed online to 2,518 people who were then asked about their intentions to make a bequest to any of 40 large national US charities. In all cases, the advertisements containing stories told by living individuals generated greater intention to donate than did the advertisements with (identical) stories related by deceased people. Therefore, the authors concluded, death should be de-emphasised in bequest fundraising.

Wiepking, Scaife, and McDonald (2012) drew hypotheses from the general fundraising literature to identity factors possibly associated with making bequests. Results from a survey of 846 people in Australia suggested that the main motives related to (i) belief in the efficacy of the recipient nonprofit, (ii) belief that the legator's family was financially well-provided for, and (iii) a person's financial ability to make a bequest. Perceptions of the difficulties involved in making a bequest also played a role. In line with these results, lack of family need was also a significant variable in Sikkel and Schoenmakers' (2012) investigation of the motives of 667 Dutch people over the age of 55 to make bequests to health-related charitable organisations. Empathy with the suffering of others was the most important explanatory variable. Empathetic concern was itself influenced by altruism and the degree to which a person was attracted to a nonprofit. Other significant considerations were participants' feelings of gratitude for being in good health themselves, and personal experience of a particular disease.

Box 4.6   Research opportunities: major gift fundraising and legacy fundraising

It can be seen from the above that research in these areas has been mostly ad hoc and without unifying frameworks. A line of enquiry that might lead to the establishment of theoretical foundations for MGF could involve a robust academic categorisation of the motives of wealthy people for making very large gifts, including bequests. Grey literature in the MGF field has offered many lists of motives attributable to major givers; but rigorous scrutiny and scientific testing of these practitioner-driven lists is required. Further opportunities for research in MGF and legacy fundraising include the examination of sources of influence on major givers, the decision processes of major givers, and the decision-making units involved. In principle, moreover, Big Data should greatly ease the administrative burden of identifying prospects (subject to national privacy laws) and of determining the best forms of approach. Research is needed into the application of digital technologies to MGF. Additionally, there is scope for investigations into the antecedents of various strategic orientations applied to MGF by disparate types of nonprofit organisation.

As regards legacy fundraising, explorations of the 'terror theories' found in the sociology literature may be useful for helping researchers overcome study participants' reluctance to discuss their attitudes and behaviour vis-à-vis making bequests. Grey literature has analysed the times in people's life cycles when they are most likely to make a will (young, middle aged, old, very old). Academic research could examine this matter in greater detail, possibly utilising psychographic segmentation.

References

Algharat, R., Rana, N., Dwivedi, Y., Alalwan, A. and Qasam, Z. (2018) "The Effect of Telepresence, Social Presence and Involvement on Consumer Brand Engagement: An Empirical Study of Nonprofit Organisations", *Journal of Retailing and Consumer Services* 40, 139–149.

Balboni, B. and Kocollari, U. (2017) "Crowdfunding for Social Enterprises: An Exploratory Analysis of the Italian Context". In Meric, J., Masque, I. and Brabat, J. (Eds), *International Perspectives on Crowdfunding*, 65–79, Bradford: Emerald Insight.

Bennett, R. (2012) "Selection of Individuals to Serve on Major Gift Fundraising Teams: A Study of Membership Choice Criteria", *International Journal of Nonprofit and Voluntary Sector Marketing* 17 (1), 49–64.

Bennett, R. (2017) "Relevance of Fundraising Charities' Content Marketing Objectives: Perceptions of Donors, Fundraisers and their Consultants", *Journal of Nonprofit and Public Sector Marketing* 29 (1), 39–63.

Bennett, R. and Kottasz, R. (2000) "Emergency Fundraising for Disaster Relief", *Disaster Prevention and Management: An International Journal* 9 (5), 352–360.

Bennett, R., Mousley, W., Kitchin, P. and Ali-Choudhury, R. (2007) "Motivations for Participating in Charity-Affiliated Sporting Events", *Journal of Customer Behaviour* 6 (2), 155–178.

Bhati, A. and McDonnell, D. (2020) "Success in an Online Giving Day: The Role of Social Media in Fundraising", *Nonprofit and Voluntary Sector Quarterly* 49 (1), 74–92.

Buskila, G. and Perez, D. (2022) "The Impact of Victims' Imagery on Charity Crowdfunding Campaigns: How Photos of Victims Doing Nothing to Help Themselves Elicit Fewer Donations", *Journal of Advertising Research* 62 (4), 385–396.

Chapman, C., Hornsey, M., Fielding, K. and Gulliver, R. (2022) "International Media Coverage Promotes Donations to a Climate Disaster", *Disasters*, Epub ahead of print.

Chen, Y., Dai, R., Wang, L., Yang, S., Li, Y. and Wei, J. (2021) "Exploring Donor's Intention in Charitable Crowdfunding: Intrinsic and Extrinsic Motivations", *Industrial Management and Data Systems* 121 (7), 1664–1683.

Choy, K. and Schlagwein, D. (2017) "Crowdsourcing for a Better World: On the Relation Between IT Affordances and Donor Motivations in Charity Crowdfunding", *Information Technology and People* 29 (1), 221–247.

Coghlan, A. and Filo, K. (2013) "Using Constant Comparison Method and Qualitative Data to Understand Participants' Experiences at the Nexus of Tourism, Sport and Charity Events", *Tourism Management* 35, 122–131.

Curtis, L., Edwards, C., Fraser, K., Gudelsky, S., Holmquist, J., Thornton, K. and Sweetser, K. (2010) "Adoption of Social Media by Nonprofit Organisations", *Public Relations Review* 36 (1), 90–92.

De Pelsmacker, P., Dens, N. and De Meulenaer, S. (2022) "The Effects of Model Ethnicity in Charity Appeals for Local and Global Charities", *Journal of Nonprofit and Public Sector Marketing* 34 (1), 129–148.

Drollinger, T. (2017) "Using Active Empathetic Listening to Build Relationships with Major Gift Donors", *Journal of Nonprofit and Public Sector Marketing* 30 (1), 37–51.

van Esch, P., Cui, Y. and Jain, S. (2021) "COVID-19 Charity Advertising: Identifiable Victim Message Framing, Self-Construal, and Donation Intent", *Journal of Advertising* 50 (3), 290–298.

Fan-Osuala, O., Zantedeschi, D. and Jank, W. (2017) "Using Past Contribution Patterns to Forecast Fundraising Outcomes in Crowdfunding", *International Journal of Forecasting* 34 (1), 30–44.

Feldman, D. and Feldman, (1985) "The Effects of a Telethon on Attitudes toward Disabled People and Financial Donations", *Journal of Rehabilitation* 51 (3), 42–53.

Filo, K., Fechner, D. and Inoue, Y. (2020) "Charity Sport Event Participants and Fundraising: An Examination of Constraints and Negotiation Strategies", *Sport Management Review* 23 (3), 387–400.

Ge, R., Zhang, S. and Zhao, H. (2022) "Do Expressions of Sadness, Anxiety and Fear have Different Impacts on Attracting Donations? Evidence from a Chinese Online Charitable Crowdfunding Platform", *Information Technology and People*, ahead-of-print.

Herrero, M. and Kraemer, S. (2022) "Beyond Survival Mode: Organizational Resilience Capabilities in Nonprofit Arts and Culture Fundraising During the Covid-19 Pandemic", *Nonprofit Management and Leadership* 33 (2), 279–295.

Jang, H. (2022) "Cuteness Mediates the Effect of Happy Facial Expressions on Empathy and Charitable Donations", *International Review on Public and Nonprofit Marketing* 19, 675–689.

Jefferess, D. (2002) "For Sale – Peace of Mind: Neo-Colonial Discourse and the Commodification of Third World Poverty in World Vision's Telethons", *Critical Arts* 16 (1), 1–15.

Jin, S. and Ryu, E. (2022) "'The Greedy I that Gives'—The Paradox of Egocentrism and Altruism: Terror Management and System Justification Perspectives on the Interrelationship Between Mortality Salience and Charitable Donations Amid the COVID-19 Pandemic", *Journal of Consumer Affairs* 56 (1), 414–448.

Knowles, P. and Gomes, R. (2009) "Building Relationships with Major Gift Donors: A Major Gift Decision-Making, Relationship-Building Model", *Journal of Nonprofit and Public Sector Marketing* 21 (4), 384–405.

Kottasz, R., MacQuillin, I. and Bennett, R. (2022) "Nonprofit and Charity Marketing: Navigating Amidst the Growing Markets for Social Conscience and Pressure for Purpose". In Kubacki, K., Parker, L., Domegan, C. and Brennan, L. (Eds), *The Routledge Companion to Marketing and Society*, 306–315, London: Routledge.

Lee, D. and Park, J. (2020) "The Relationship Between a Charity Crowdfunding Project's Contents and Donors' Participation: An Empirical Study with Deep Learning Methodologies", *Computers in Human Behaviour* 106, 106261.

Leventhal, D. and Foot, C. (2015) "The Relationship Between Disclosure and Household Donations to Nonprofit Organisations in Australia", *Nonprofit and Voluntary Sector Quarterly* 45 (5), 992–1012.

Li, B., Hou, F., Guan, Z. and Chong, A. (2022) "The Use of Social Media for a Better World: Roles of Social Experience, Empathy and Personal Impulsiveness in Charitable Crowdfunding", *Information Technology and People*, ahead-of-print.

Li, M. and Yin, C. (2022) "Facial Expressions of Beneficiaries and Donation Intentions of Potential Donors: Effects of the Number of Beneficiaries in Charity Advertising", *Journal of Retailing and Consumer Services*, 66, 102915.

Liu, L, Suh, A. and Wagner, C. (2017) "Donation Behaviour in Online Micro Charities: An Investigation of Charitable Crowdfunding Projects". In *Proceedings of the 50th Hawaii International Conference on System Science*, Hawaii: AISel. Accessed 22 November 2017 at www.aisel.aisnet.org.

Longmore, P. (2005) "The Cultural Framing of Disability: Telethons", *Publications of the Modern Language Association of America* 120 (2), 502–508.

Lovejoy, K. and Saxton, G. (2012) "Information, Community, and Action: How Nonprofit Organisations Use Social Media", *Journal of Computer-Mediated Communication* 17 (3), 337–353.

Lovejoy, K., Waters, R. and Saxton, G. (2012) "Engaging Stakeholders through Twitter: How Nonprofit Organisations are Getting More Out of 140 Characters or Less", *Public Relations Review* 38 (2), 313–318.

Mayo, J. (2021) "How Do Big Gifts Affect Rival Charities and Their Donors?", *Journal of Economic Behaviour and Organization* 191, 575–597.

Mendini, M., Peter, P. and Maione, S. (2022) "The Potential Positive Effects of Time Spent on Instagram on Consumers' Gratitude, Altruism, and Willingness to Donate", *Journal of Business Research*, 143, 16–26.

Mezinska, S., Kakuk, P., Mijaljica, G., Waligóra, M. and O'Mathúna, D. (2016) "Research in Disaster Settings: A Systematic Qualitative Review of Ethical Guidelines, *BMC Medical Ethics* 17, 62.

Pham, C. and Septianto, F. (2019), "A Smile – the Key to Everybody's Heart? The Interactive Effects of Image and Message in Increasing Charitable Behaviour", *European Journal of Marketing* 54 (2), 261–281.

Pressgrove, G., McKeever, B. and Jang, S. (2018) "What is Contagious? Exploring Why Content Goes Viral on Twitter: A Case Study of the ALS Ice Bucket Challenge", *International Journal of Nonprofit and Voluntary Sector Marketing* 23 (1), e1586.

Russell, J. and Routley, C. (2016) "We the Living: The Effects of Living and Deceased Donor Stories on Charitable Bequest Giving Intentions", *International Journal of Nonprofit and Voluntary Sector Marketing* 21 (2), 109–117.

Sargeant, A., Eisenstein, A. and Kottasz, R. (2015) *Major Gift Fundraising: Unlocking the Potential for Smaller Nonprofits*, Plymouth: Centre for Sustainable Philanthropy, Plymouth University.

Sargeant, A. and Lee, S. (2004) "Trust and Relationship Commitment in the United Kingdom Voluntary Sector: Determinants of Donor Behaviour", *Psychology and Marketing* 21 (8), 613–635.

Saxton, G. and Wang, L. (2014) "The Social Network Effect", *Nonprofit and Voluntary Sector Quarterly* 43 (5), 850–868.

Sepehri, A., Duclos, R., Kristofferson, K., Vinoo, P. and Elahi, H. (2021) "The Power of Indirect Appeals in Peer-to-Peer Fundraising: Why 'S/He' Can Raise More Money for Me Than 'I' Can for Myself", *Journal of Consumer Psychology* 31 (3), 612–620.

Shin, N. (2019) "The Impact of the Web and Social Media on the Performance of Nonprofit Organizations," *Journal of International Technology and Information Management* 27 (4), Article 2.

Sikkel, D. and Schoenmakers, E. (2012) "Bequests to Health-Related Charitable Organisations: A Structural Model", *International Journal of Nonprofit and Voluntary Sector Marketing* 17 (3), 183–197.

Sisson, D. (2017) "Control Mutuality, Social Media, and Organisation-Public Relationships: A Study of Local Animal Welfare Organisations", *Public Relations Review* 43 (1), 179–189.

Stiver, A., Barroca, L. and Minocha, S. (2015) "Civic Crowdfunding Research: Opportunities and Challenges", *New Media and Society* 17 (2), 249–271.

Szper, R. and Prakash, A. (2011) "Charity Watchdogs and the Limits of Information Based Regulation", *Voluntas* 22 (1), 112–141.

Wallace, E., Buil, I. and de Chernatony, L. (2017). "When Does 'Liking' a Charity Lead to Donation Behaviour? Exploring Conspicuous Donation Behaviour on Social Media Platforms", *European Journal of Marketing* 51 (11/12), 2002–2029.

Waters, R. (2013) "Tracing the Impact of Media Relations and Television Coverage on US Charitable Relief Fundraising: An Application of Agenda-Setting Theory Across Three Natural Disasters", *Journal of Public Relations Research* 25 (4), 329–346.

Waters, R., Burnett, E., Lamm, A. and Lucas, J. (2009) "Engaging Stakeholders through Social Networking: How Nonprofit Organisations are Using Facebook", *Public Relations Review* 35 (2), 102–106.

Wiepking, P., Scaife, W. and McDonald, K. (2012) "Motives and Barriers to Bequest Giving", *Journal of Consumer Behaviour* 11 (1), 56–66.

Wilks, L. (2016) "Communicating an Arts Foundation's Values: Sights, Sounds and Social Media", *Arts and the Market* 6 (2), 206–223.

Won, D. and Park, M. (2010) "Motivating Factors Influencing College Students' Participation in Charity Sporting Events", *International Journal of Sport Management and Marketing* 8 (3/4), 296–321.

Woolf, J., Heere, B. and Walker, M. (2013) "Do Charity Sports Events Function as 'Brandfests' in the Development of Brand Community?", *Journal of Sport Management* 27, 95–107.

Wymer, W. and Čačija, L. (2022) "Online Social Network Fundraising: Threats and Potentialities", *Journal of Philanthropy and Marketing*, early view website.

Xiao, A., Huang, Y., Bortree, D. and Waters, R. (2022) "Designing Social Media Fundraising Messages: An Experimental Approach to Understanding how Message Concreteness and Framing Influence Donation Intentions", *Nonprofit and Voluntary Sector Quarterly* 51 (4), 832–856.

Xue, F. and Zhou, L. (2022) "Understanding Social Influence in Facebook Fundraising: Relationship Strength, Immediacy of Needs, and Number of Donations", *Journal of Philanthropy and Marketing*, Early View.

Zheng, C., Niu, H. and Wang, H. (2023) "No Browsing, No Donating: The Impact of Title and Forwarder on Browsing Intention of Online Charity Fundraising", *International Review on Public and Nonprofit Marketing*, Early view.

Zhou, L. and Xue, F. (2019) "Effects of Colour in Disaster Relief Advertising and the Mediating Role of Cognitive Elaboration", *Journal of Nonprofit and Public Sector Marketing* 31 (4), 403–427.

Zong, Z. and Lin, S. (2017) "The Antecedents and Consequences of Charitable Donation Heterogeneity on Social Media", *International Journal of Nonprofit and Voluntary Sector Marketing* 23 (1), e1585.

5 Conclusion, reflections, and opportunities for future research

Research within the fundraising and nonprofit marketing domain has examined a wide range of topics, both empirically and conceptually. However, many studies in the field have explored issues through the lenses of other academic disciplines (economics, social psychology, public policy, anthropology, organisational behaviour, etc.), leading to allegations that fundraising and nonprofit marketing does not, as a subject, possess a set of theories that unify the field. Accusations concerning the paucity of theory within fundraising and nonprofit marketing research have not escaped attention in academic circles; and many editorials in academic nonprofit journals, in the Forewords to Special Issues on nonprofit marketing appearing in the more general marketing journals, and in Calls for Papers for submissions to international nonprofit marketing conferences have lamented the absence of theoretical infrastructures in substantial areas of nonprofit marketing research. Without doubt, studies in fundraising and nonprofit marketing have examined a plethora of ad hoc practical and utilitarian topics and have frequently investigated just a single element of an issue, e.g., the wording of an appeal, a particular reason for making a gift, a certain advertising format, or a specific personality trait. It is perhaps unsurprising, therefore, that nonprofit and fundraising research is often seen as diverse and fragmented, with investigators paying less attention to matters of theory than occurs in most other academic disciplines.

Arguably, however, the fundamental explanation of the diverse, fragmented, and allegedly theoretically deficient nature of fundraising and nonprofit marketing research is, quite simply, that the area *itself* is diverse, fragmented, and not amenable to theory development. Within the nonprofit and fundraising domain a 'what works' philosophy may often comprise the best approach when researching a topic, but this does not mean that theoretical matters are unimportant or that they are routinely ignored by nonprofit researchers. Indeed, the diversity of the subject matter of fundraising and nonprofit marketing has, by its very nature, the capacity to engender rich research agendas that are both practically useful *and* amenable to robust academic investigation. It is relevant to note, nevertheless, that theory construction

DOI: 10.4324/9781003364405-5

in fundraising and nonprofit marketing can be difficult due to (i) the presence of high levels of causal complexity in the subject matter of issues under investigation and in their surrounding environments (socioeconomic, political, regulatory, etc.) and (ii) the fact that many of the topics of interest in nonprofit and fundraising research cannot easily be separated from practical concerns, especially issues involving human welfare. Also, the (purportedly slow) pace of theory development in the fundraising and nonprofit marketing area may have been affected by the fast-changing nature of the fundraising and nonprofit marketing milieu, as the presence of constant change could have exerted a constraining influence on the consideration of theoretical issues.

Critics have asserted, nonetheless, that while studies completed with few theoretical underpinnings have offered solutions to down-to-earth problems, the proliferation of 'investigations without theory' has led to an abundance of research outcomes that are neither (i) generalisable for operational purposes nor (ii) theoretically useful in other academic domains. A paper that illustrated the demand that nonprofit researchers pay greater attention to theoretical matters was authored by Wymer (2013), whose review of criticisms of nonprofit marketing and fundraising research reported claims that the nonprofit research area suffered flaws relating to (i) inconsistent definitions of core constructs, (ii) few replications of studies, (iii) frequent applications of weak scientific methods, (iv) numerous impromptu in-situ theory constructions, and (v) naive uses of theories drawn from social psychology. Further negative assertions about nonprofit marketing noted in Wymer's (2013) literature review included accusations that there was no consensus regarding the foundations of the subject, no *unified* critical mass of scholarship within the domain, and too many studies that did little more than change a single variable in an existing model. Although several of these accusations are unfounded, nonprofit researchers should be cognisant of their existence and wherever possible should address them in the course of their work.

An interesting and valuable contribution to the debate on the role of theory in nonprofit marketing was contained in a paper by Taylor, Torugsa, and Arundel (2017), who argued for the adoption of 'abduction approaches' when conducting nonprofit research. An abduction approach begins with an observation and then seeks its simplest and most likely explanation. Abduction begins with an 'educated guess' as the most likely hypotheses to use in a study. It involves the use of inferences to obtain explanations, as opposed to 'deduction' where initial premises substantially predetermine a conclusion, and 'induction' where general conclusions are drawn from specific instances (as typically occurs following experimentation). Deductive reasoning has been criticised for lack of clarity vis-à-vis the selection of the theories that are to be employed to explain phenomena, while inductive reasoning has been censured for the unreliability of theories built on incomplete information. Advocates of the abductive approach note that it is routinely applied within research studies in several scientific disciplines and is the predominant mode of reasoning in medical diagnosis. Abduction, according to Taylor et al. (2017), facilitates the formulation of testable exploratory hypotheses for nonprofit issues in a 'sensory and logically structured way' (p. 1) and constitutes a practice-led research method which has the potential to bridge the practitioner scholar divide. Problems with abduction are that the explanations resulting from its application may be false or inadequate, given that conclusions drawn from the process might not follow logically from observed events. In particular, directions of causality might be the reverse of those initially assumed. Also, theory derived from an abductive approach might in reality be nested within a wider theory that an abductive investigation has ignored. It can be the case, moreover, that the dividing line between adduction and other forms of inference become blurred.

A more general approach to the application of theoretical frameworks to nonprofit marketing was offered by Novatorov (2018), who advocated the adoption of the 'Pluralistic Methodological Paradigm' as the most effective way of improving the quality of nonprofit investigations. Methodological pluralism proposes that all approaches (positivist, interpretivist, critical theory, etc.) 'have a right to coexist because they generate different types of knowledge' (p. 68). Noting the prevalence of the positivist–empiricist paradigm in most nonprofit marketing research (an approach that emphasises prediction based on scientific methods and nomological explanation), The author argued that findings from positivist studies should be triangulated in order to take account of 'values that contribute to the conservation of existing social conditions' (p. 71). By simultaneously examining an issue from more than one theoretical viewpoint, triangulation of research approaches would, Navatorov (2018) continued, explain more fully the richness and complexity of human behaviour. Otherwise, findings from an investigation might be forced to fit into a particular theory, hence closing discussion on any aspect of the issue that did not fall within the remit of the theory selected.

Future research in fundraising and nonprofit marketing

The sparsity of the theoretical underpinnings of many studies in the fundraising and nonprofit marketing area needs to be acknowledged yet, as previous chapters have demonstrated, a substantial and valuable body of literature involving the subject now exists. Frameworks for understanding the multiple facets of fundraising have been developed (see Chapter 2), and several streams of compelling research have emerged. Vexing and recurring questions in the fundraising and nonprofit marketing field (e.g., mission drift, the relatively modest giving behaviour of the wealthy, and the consequences of the negative framing of charity advertisements) continue to be addressed, and fresh approaches to resolving these questions are being explored. As well as providing opportunities to examine particular issues, the fundraising and nonprofit marketing discipline will, as it matures, offer numerous fresh opportunities for critically examining the roots of the subject and the general directions it should follow.

Publication opportunities are available for fundraising and nonprofit marketing scholars in a number of outlets. Currently, three well-established academic journals are dedicated to the subject, i.e., the *International Journal of Nonprofit and Voluntary Sector Marketing* (renamed as the *Journal of Philanthropy and Marketing*), the *Journal of Nonprofit and Public Sector Marketing*, and the *International Review on Public and Nonprofit Marketing*. Additionally, articles on nonprofit marketing and fundraising regularly appear in the journals titled *Nonprofit and Voluntary Sector Quarterly*, *Voluntas: International Journal of Voluntary and Nonprofit Organisations*, *Nonprofit Management and Leadership*, and in the journal *Social Business*. General marketing journals (e.g., the *Journal of Marketing Management*, the *International Journal of Research in Marketing*, the *European Journal of Marketing*, the *Journal of Marketing Theory and Practice*, *Psychology and Marketing*, and the *Journal of Business Research*) also carry articles on fundraising and nonprofit marketing. Most of the major international conferences on marketing now include nonprofit marketing tracks.

Suggested directions and topics

Academic research into fundraising and nonprofit marketing is important because, ultimately, it has the capacity to help fundraising managers obtain the financial donations necessary to maintain the philanthropic operations of nonprofit organisations. Research within the domain could become increasingly necessary, moreover, in view of the apparent preference of a growing number of Western governments for social services (and sometimes for public goods) to be supplied by nonprofits rather than by state agencies. (Chapter 1 discusses how a country's 'welfare gap' may sometimes be assuaged via government contract work undertaken by nonprofits.) Many research opportunities arise concerning the interfaces between governments and countries' nonprofit sectors, e.g., examination of nonprofits' orientations in relation to contract work for state agencies (akin perhaps to the development of scales for measuring market orientation or brand orientation); the exploration of public attitudes towards fundraising nonprofits' connections with state agencies; and the study of personal relationships and the consequences of interactions among individual fundraisers and government officials. It could well be that very few donors are aware that some of the nonprofit organisations to which they give money are heavily engaged in government contract work. If donors become aware of this situation, might they alter their attitudes and behaviour towards these nonprofits? Research designed to help answer this question would be welcome.

Further issues in fundraising and nonprofit marketing that merit future research are as follows:

1   A topic prominent in the general marketing literature but which (at the time of writing) has yet to be examined by nonprofit academics is that of 'agile marketing'. An *agile* nonprofit would be one that quickly identified new trends, developed dynamic capabilities, and flexibly imitated any successful methods and strategies introduced by competitors. The organisation would consciously acquire learning skills and be willing to alter its course of action rapidly and effectively. Research into fundraising nonprofits' abilities to become agile and the consequences of agility for fundraising performance would contribute significantly to knowledge in the nonprofit marketing field. Is agility connected with, for example, market orientation? What sorts of staff training are required to promote agility within a nonprofit and how best might training be provided? Comparisons of agile marketing behaviour in the nonprofit sector with agile activities among commercial businesses would be worthwhile.

2   Research has sought to measure the effects of economic downturns on aggregate donations to fundraising nonprofits. However, little attention has been devoted to assessing possible differences in the effects of economic cycles on specific nonprofit sectors and on nonprofits with particular characteristics. For instance, does austerity have a lower impact on charities which traditionally have been supported mainly by the financially well-off; as opposed to organisations with a donor base found mainly among the poor? What are the best fundraising strategies for accommodating large swings in a national business cycle within various nonprofit sectors? How closely do cycles in total donations to particular sectors match cycles in a national economy, and what explains differences?

3   An issue worthy of investigation is the determination of a potential donor's 'initial consideration set' regarding the choice of the particular nonprofit within a sector (cancer care for example) to which the individual will then donate. An initial consideration set is the subset of organisations that a person considers the first time the individual contemplates giving to a certain type of cause. Consideration sets come into existence because people have limited capacities to process information and need therefore to restrict the range of options they consider. For instance, will a person include only large and well-known international charities in the initial consideration set, or do other criteria apply, and if so, what are the decision factors? This matter may be especially pertinent in today's digital milieu given the large amounts of information readily available from online sources. Thus, it may be appropriate to explore the sorts of nonprofit websites that people look at online when deciding their initial consideration sets and, when they browse websites, the factors they consider when selecting specific nonprofits for incorporation in a set? What are the antecedents of disparities

among individuals in the amounts of cognitive effort they apply when determining an initial consideration set and when making a final decision? This issue should not be confused with 'top of the mind' awareness, i.e., the first nonprofit that comes to mind when thinking about a particular category of nonprofits. Research into the determinants of top of the mind awareness in the nonprofit sector would itself be useful. For instance, do disparities in top of the mind awareness vis-à-vis the first organisation that comes to mind occur with respect to groups of donors exhibiting certain characteristics. Is the organisation in question typically large, small, related to personal experience, influenced by social norms, etc.?

4   It is obviously desirable that the major outcomes to nonprofit academic research become known to practising fundraising managers, and hence that the results of academic investigations impact beneficially on fundraisers' day-to-day activities. Yet, fundraising practitioners are often sceptical of the contributions of the outputs of academic research to their everyday work. Unfortunately, moreover, even a cursory examination of the (voluminous) grey literature on fundraising available on the Internet reveals large and disturbing differences between the subject matter of articles published in academic journals and the contents of the Internet-based grey literature on fundraising and nonprofit marketing (e.g., consultants' reports, blogs, bulletins, commentaries and critiques, 'how-to-do' advice articles, short opinion pieces) that nonprofit marketing managers actually read. This is especially true vis-à-vis digital fundraising (see below).

Grey literature transmits fresh ideas and descriptions of new fundraising methods, many of which never appear in the academic domain. Problems with grey literature include the absence of quality control, the transitory nature of sources (as websites can close with the consequent loss of information), and the subjectivity and possible unreliability of the materials posted (since grey literature is rarely grounded in proven facts). Nevertheless, practitioners may trust grey literature to far greater extents that they trust academic publications, and surveys have revealed that few practitioners read academic journals.

Clearly, research into the academic–practitioner divide within the fundraising and nonprofit marketing domain would be valuable. For example, where and how do new practitioner ideas originate and develop, and how widely and enthusiastically are they taken up? Assuming that it is in fact the case that most practitioners shy away from academic literature, what are the causes of their dislike? Do practitioners find academic marketing literature too difficult to follow, too vague, too abstract, or (disturbingly from an academic point of view) largely irrelevant to their operations? What, if any, are the differences in educational background between academic nonprofit researchers and fundraising managers and, to the extent that differences exist, do such disparities help determine the latter's use of academic literature?

5   Robust historical research into the corporate philanthropy activities of Victorian owners of large businesses (e.g., George Cadbury, Lord Leverhulme, or Joseph Rowntree) or of early nineteenth-century business leaders such as John Rockefeller and Andrew Carnegie would add greatly to knowledge in the fundraising domain. Equally worthwhile would be studies of corporate philanthropy exercised by the medieval craft guilds and their early successors. It is certainly *not* the case that corporate philanthropy, cause-related marketing, and sponsorships of nonprofits began in the mid- to late twentieth century, as some contemporary literature implies.

Digitalisation: prospects and possibilities

The future of fundraising and nonprofit marketing is digital. New digital technologies are pervading every aspect of nonprofit fundraising work and (if they have not already done so) all fundraising nonprofits will need to retool for the digital age. Many nonprofit organisations are at the forefront of the use of new fundraising technologies, and academic research into how these organisations utilise the latest digital fundraising methods is required. A useful contribution in the area was a paper by Cipriano and Za (2021), which sought to develop a taxonomy based on a systematic overview of literature which has examined digital transformation in nonprofit organisations over recent decades. The work constituted the initial step of a research project aiming to investigate the impact of digital transformation on nonprofit organisations in general. A total of 111 papers were included in the study, which identified five dimensions relating to the matter: the objectives of nonprofit digitalisation, its scope and relevance to nonprofit operations, the features of digital technology, and financial aims where digitalisation was concerned. Vogelsang, Packmohr, and Brink (2021) compared the manners in which nonprofits and commercial organisations have managed digitalisation. Barriers had interfered with digitalisation in both sectors, and it was essential that barriers were recognised in order to decide on countermeasures. Sixty-seven articles on the subject were examined and 56 interviews conducted with commercial and nonprofit sector managers. Digitalisation among nonprofits had been slow, due in part to nonprofits taking the view that digitalisation was not a process in which they were actually involved. This might have been due, the authors suggested, to limited perspectives among individual managers of nonprofit organisations. Also, nonprofits often depended on volunteers whose training in digital matters was less extensive and less actively controlled than in businesses. Hence, nonprofits had to work on their recruitment of volunteers possessing digital skills in order to accelerate the pace of digitalisation in the nonprofit sector. Vogelsang et al. (2021) noted the possibility of the emergence of a 'digital divide' between nonprofits and their increasingly tech-savvy donors.

Artificial intelligence, Big Data, and fundraising research

The subject of artificial intelligence (AI) appears regularly and prominently in the grey nonprofit literature but, at the time of writing, it has rarely figured in academic nonprofit research. Some authorities have predicted that, within a couple of decades, around 80% of a typical person's interactions with organisations will occur through equipment that uses AI rather than through humans. The term AI refers to computers that undertake complex processes (often completing difficult tasks more effectively than people) and which independently learn from experience and improve their capabilities. AI computers learn via artificial neural networks that mimic human-like trial-and-error learning.

An AI computer can learn about donors from a huge and constantly expanding database of messages received by a fundraising nonprofit from its supporters and from prospective donors, and will learn how to respond in the most effective ways. The machine will be able to initiate a two-way conversation with a prospective donor using email, text, or social media; having learned how to do this from a bank of phrases put together in advance. AI machines can detect patterns, connections, and relationships within data, and can identify any number of customer personas. Relevant pre-scheduled communications may then be targeted at micro-segments. Machine learning will also play an increasingly important role in determining charity fundraising operations in future years. For example, a fundamental issue for charities is how to maximise the probability of receiving a donation from a particular individual. When charities make data-driven decisions, they typically rely on the donation history of a donor. Lee, Veera Raghavan, and Hobbs (2020) examined possibilities for predicting a person's next donation, using a sample charity's time-series data, and demonstrated that based on a donor's previous five actions, the likely donation amount of a sixth action could be approximated. The authors argued that Recurrent Neural Networks could accurately model how much a person will donate. (Neural networks are computer systems that mimic the human brain, learning from data and finding patterns.) Cagala, Glogowsky, Rincke, and Strittmatter (2021) developed a machine learning procedure for 'optimally' targeting individuals whose expected donations exceeded solicitation costs. To use the procedure a charity only required publicly available geospatial information. The system assumed that individuals who had previously been asked but had never donated should not be targeted. Otherwise, resources would be wasted.

AI facilitated by Big Data will create numerous opportunities for nonprofits to improve their fundraising performance and hence will offer many avenues for productive and innovative fundraising research. A report submitted to the UK government by Davies and Pickering (2017) on behalf of the UK Charities Aid Foundation observed how Big Data could access up to 5000 data points on every UK citizen, and thus made possible the detailed micro-segmentation of the entire nonprofit donation market. Big Data could, Davies and Pickering (2017) continued, be used by an AI installation for 'behavioural targeting', i.e., the simultaneous delivery of thousands of variants of message content optimised to influence individual people. Through creating emotionally intelligent communications in real time and by crafting personalised donor-centric communications without human intervention, an AI computer connected to Big Data could itself manage relationships with donors. Lv and Huang, M. (2022) observed that charities have increasingly used personalised recommendations in their fundraising advertising, where the recommendations were powered by AI. The effectiveness of charity advertising could improve through using AI although, the authors suggested, there was evidence that personalised recommendations in charity advertising may have a dark side. To test this, Lv and Huang (2022) completed five studies using student and non-student samples varying in size from 70 to 203 individuals, finding that people exhibited lower donation intentions when they received charity advertising with (versus without) personalised recommendations. Based on self-determination theory, this result was posited to be due to a decrease in perceived personal autonomy. Personalised recommendations in charity advertising could decrease donation intentions by partly disturbing donors' decisions and destroying their perceived autonomy during the donation process.

An AI application increasingly used in the commercial sector is that of 'sympathy mining' (also known as sentiment mining), i.e., the analysis of the content of social media messages that have been posted online with the aim of identifying opinions and feelings within target donor segments. The main social media platforms now offer basic sentiment mining facilities, and more sophisticated and customised sentiment mining services are available from specialist consultancies. Some sentiment mining activities can be undertaken manually by employees of fundraising organisations, but AI can analyse the sentiment aspects of interactions with donors faster, more accurately, and less expensively than has previously been possible using humans. 'Deep learning' by AI equipment about donors' lifestyles, behaviour, and preferences (via the use of large neural networks) can help fundraisers to refine and better-target appeals.

Chat bots will be able to provide potential donors with tailored information about a nonprofit 24 hours a day, seven days a week. Two studies by Baek, Bakpayev, Yoon, and Kim (2022) (one with 240 non-student participants, the other using 127 undergraduates) demonstrated that when nonprofit charity marketers designed AI agents to resemble humans and to smile like humans (rather than like robots), potential donors felt psychologically closer to the agents and in consequence were motivated to increase their charitable giving. The broader the AI agent's smile the more effective the interaction.

Clearly, academic research can contribute in several ways to knowledge concerning the impact of AI on fundraising. An obvious and pressing research task is to map the emerging fundraising and nonprofit marketing AI terrain. Particular issues that AI-related research could help resolve include:

- How best to integrate an AI strategy into a nonprofit's overall fundraising strategies;
- Whether new governance structures are needed by nonprofits that implement extensive AI and Big Data systems;
- Whether it is possible for donors to engage with communications created by AI to the same extent as with communications initiated by humans, and whether potential donors are willing to deal with AI agents;
- How the effects of replies to donors' queries given by chat bots compare with the effects of replies given by humans;
- The determination of the fundraising tasks that can be taken over by AI, e.g., scheduling, targeting, identifying trends, and assessing performance levels;
- How to overcome the problems and potential pitfalls connected with the introduction of AI;
- How to identify the skills that fundraising managers will need to acquire to implement AI-based systems.

Apart from AI, some of the topics that warrant research in the more general digital marketing field are as follows:

- Predicting the online fundraising world *beyond* social media (considering that click rates for fundraising nonprofits on social media platforms have declined, presumably as a consequence of saturation of the fundraising market);
- Finding ways of embedding nonprofits into the Internet of Things, thus enabling people to donate via a range of connected objects;
- Measuring in real-time donors' emotions while viewing online fundraising appeals;
- Determining the best types of stories to include in mobile marketing appeals;
- Assessing the utility of extreme micro-segmentation. Much research effort has been devoted to segmenting donor markets. Segmentation is only worthwhile, however, if it *actually* drives greater donations. Case studies of scenarios where segmentation is inappropriate, even counter-productive, would be worthwhile.

Some personal reflections

Notwithstanding the alleged theoretical shortcomings of research into nonprofit marketing and fundraising outlined in previous sections, scholarly research in the fundraising and nonprofit marketing domain has produced a substantial and valuable body of findings, suggestions, propositions, and recommendations that fundraising managers can profitably use in their work. Moreover, some recent research has (usefully) explored the methodologies employed in fundraising investigations. Bhati and Hansen (2020), for example, commented on an upsurge in the application of experimental studies within the fundraising domain that has occurred in recent decades. Experimental research is, the authors contended, a worthwhile method for testing competing explanations and for establishing (rather than assuming) causality because it typically exhibits academic rigour and is subject to a researcher's control. Thus, Bhati and Hansen (2020) argued, experimentation has much to offer with respect to the theorisation and practice of fundraising. Interestedly, the authors' analysis of 187 experimental research articles relating to fundraising appearing in academic journals across diverse disciplines between 2007 and 2019 found that 40% were published in economics journals, and that disciplines other than fundraising were well-represented. This raises the question of why researchers who complete fundraising-related experimental studies have tended not to publish in specialist nonprofit fundraising journals. In the main, the experimental studies examined by Bhati and Hansen (2020) omitted all ethical aspects of fundraising. Clearly, more experimentation is needed in mainstream fundraising research.

Case study research has also been recommended as a valuable means for helping to establish causality, given that case studies involve detailed and in-depth data collection from multiple sources, explore contexts and cultures, and recognise the importance of social realities. However, there are problems with case study research. Examples relate to possible data overload, the intrusion of unintended biases, and lack of generalisability due to context-specific findings. (See Alborough and Hansen [2022] for a discussion of these issues.) In practice, much fundraising research has employed quantitative techniques. Kumar and Chakrabarti's (2023) review of 97 charity fundraising articles which were based on quantitative methodologies revealed that 63 had employed regression analysis, 18 had applied factor analysis, and 16 had used structural equation modelling. This suggests the widespread use within nonprofit fundraising studies of a narrow range of quantitative research methods. The employment of a broader range of approaches might greatly improve the reliability of findings. For instance, Martinez-Levy, Rossi, Cartocci et al. (2022) commented on the paucity of techniques such as neuromarketing and eye-tracking to investigate the effectiveness of nonprofit fundraising appeals (in contrast to the growth of commercial interest in these methods). As regards the geographical locations of studies, Jung, Kim and Suh's (2022) surveyed 140 articles relating to the nonprofit sector that were published between 2000 and 2019 finding that 127 involved single-nation research, of which 48% were conducted in North America (mostly the USA) and 24% in Europe (mainly the UK). It seems that research in nonprofit fundraising is based mostly on

Western perspectives, raising serious questions about the international generalisability of findings.

A highly problematic issue that needs to be addressed is the above mentioned disconnect between academic research and practitioner activity. This
cannot be permitted to widen if fundraising and nonprofit marketing research

---

**Box 5.1   Research opportunities: methodology of
fundraising and nonprofit marketing research**

Although the methodologies employed within studies of nonprofit marketing and fundraising have become more robust and rigorous in recent
years, more consideration still needs to be given to methodological
issues in fundraising research. As occurs in other disciplines (psychology and industrial marketing management for example) it would be
useful for nonprofit journals to publish occasional surveys of recently
developed (and of some older) research methods relevant for fundraising investigations. The quality of datasets used in nonprofit studies is
worthy of investigation, as are the techniques commonly employed in
small-scale experiments. Should the triangulation of results be a formal requirement of a study, and how large a sample is necessary for
reliable experimentation? (Triangulation involves the application of
more than one kind of method to study a phenomenon and is known to
be beneficial in providing confirmation of findings, increased validity
and enhanced understanding of results.) Several matters are worthy of
investigation in relation to extant research in the fundraising and nonprofit field. For instance, how common has been the (arguably naive)
application of simple linear models in cross-sectional studies? How
often has causality been assumed rather than tested using mixed methods? How many published articles have exposed theories to stringent
analysis and have attempted to falsify past findings? To what extent
have nonprofit researchers failed to recognise 'the illusion of methodological imperfection' and thus have paid insufficient attention to a
study's limitations? Often, nonprofit researchers employ measurement
instruments originally created by authors working in the for-profit academic research area, frequently without alteration. Is this acceptable,
or should nonprofit research always develop its own purpose-built survey instruments? Previous chapters have shown that fundraising studies have employed a very wide range of antecedent variables. It is not
possible to include all of them in future investigations, so what criteria should be applied to decide which variables are relevant for what
research purposes?

is to be regarded as credible, relevant, meaningful, impactful, and (crucially) worthy of state and/or internal university financial support. Another pressing difficulty is that a considerable degree of confusion seems to exist among nonprofit researchers regarding the appropriate uses of the terms 'theory', 'model', 'proposition', and 'hypothesis'. Epistemologists differ (sometimes contentiously) in their interpretations of these terms, but there does appear to be a consensus that a theory *explains* a phenomenon whereas a model *represents* a theory and thus provides an understanding of the theory. A hypothesis is an *assumption* to be tested; a proposition is a framework upon which a hypothesis is based. Opinions can differ as to whether hypotheses precede a theory or are derived from a theory. Whatever configuration of terms is appropriate, nonprofit researchers often employ these terms loosely and interchangeably; resulting in conceptual imprecision and questionable directions of causality when constructing models. Unfortunately, moreover, a number of researchers in the nonprofit marketing field (as well as in other disciplines) wrongly associate 'methodology' with 'theory', thus conflating two entirely different entities. An excellent innovation would be the introduction of common methodological frameworks and terminologies for nonprofit research, as occurs in a number of scientific disciplines. This would enable nonprofit academics to standardise the findings of their work and to compare the results of one investigation with the outcomes to others. (A useful discussion of the meaning of 'theory' in the context of marketing is contained in an article by Hunt [2011].)

A third problem with research in fundraising and nonprofit marketing is that a large number of papers employ donation *intention* rather than actual donation as the dependent variable, but without further investigating or even discussing whether intention is likely to lead to actual behaviour. The usefulness of employing donation intention as a variable to be explained is unclear. Some investigations of this matter have shown significant correlations between intended and actual donation, but the magnitudes of correlations have not been impressive (typically explaining between 20% and 40% of total variance). Shang, Sargeant, and Carpenter (2019) analysed a data set of more than 17,000 donors to five large charities to see whether the relationships between satisfaction, trust, commitment and giving intention were the same as for actual giving behaviour. The authors found that these three independent variables affected both intentions to give and actual giving, but that their impacts were between three and eight times higher in models for giving intention than for giving behaviour. Much deeper research is required into the donation intention–behaviour link, considering the fact that investigations into connections between intention and behaviour in more general contexts (e.g., purchases of products) have revealed that complex influences affect the presumed link (see Armitage and Connor, 2001 for information on relevant studies). A valuable paper by Bekkers (2005) examined or alluded to a number of the variables that might affect the donation intention–behaviour relationship, e.g., levels of altruism and empathy among donors, interest in a cause, beliefs in a nonprofit's efficiency, irritation with a fundraiser's communications, people's tendencies to overestimate their own generosity, involvement with general charity giving. However, apart from Bekkers' (2005) contribution, research on the subject within the donor behaviour domain has been sparse. Several matters require investigation in the area. How, for example, might the characteristics of the intention–behaviour link vary with respect to (i) the ways in which potential donors are approached, (ii) the amounts of money requested, (iii) the mode of ask (mobile, social media, etc.), and (iv) how easily a person can make a donation. How might measurement issues bias the results of studies of donation intention versus actual giving, e.g., if asking people to remember how much they actually donated causes them to overestimate the amount, or if asking individuals whether they intend to give actually stimulates additional giving?

The next difficulty is the seemingly endemic use of student samples within studies, especially in small-sample laboratory-based experiments that examine the influences on donation attitudes and intentions of just one or two prosaic moderating or mediating variables. Journal editors, reviewers and others who evaluate research articles might perhaps reflect more acutely on the usefulness of papers based on methodologies of this type. Assembling a control group of 'conventional' potential donors drawn from the general public does not require a great deal of effort, and the validation of results obtained from student samples against outcomes from a control group of 'typical' non-student participants can greatly enhance the reliability of the results of a student-based investigation.

A fifth problematic issue affecting the future of nonprofit and fundraising research concerns the questionable status of the subject in the eyes of government and university funders. An important consequence of greater nonprofit provision of welfare services that previously were supplied by the state (see Chapter 1) will, among other things, be a rise in the demand both for well-trained professional fundraisers and competent academic researchers in the field. Governments in many countries have encouraged nonprofits to expand and to contribute more to civil society. Yet, in the same countries, state funding of scholarly research into nonprofit fundraising has often failed to keep pace with the growth of the scale and significance of a nation's nonprofit sector. There is, therefore, a strong case for substantial increases in state investment in nonprofit research in countries that possess significant civil societies.

An apology

This book must end with an apology. The fundraising and nonprofit marketing field is fast changing, and it is inevitable therefore that during the course of my writing this book, I may have missed some newly published and valuable contributions. I regret any significant omissions; responsibility for which is mine alone.

References

Alborough, L. and Hansen, R. (2022) "Reframing Fundraising Research: The Challenges and Opportunities of Interpretivist Research Practices and Practitioner Researchers in Fundraising Studies", *Journal of Philanthropy and Marketing*, e1775.

Armitage, C. and Connor, M. (2001) "Efficacy of the Theory of Planned Behaviour", *British Journal of Social Psychology* 40, 471–499.

Baek, T., Bakpayev, M., Yoon, S. and Kim, S. (2022) "Smiling AI Agents: How Anthropomorphism and Broad Smiles increase Charitable Giving", *International Journal of Advertising* 41 (5), 850–867.

Bekkers, R (2005) *Words and Deeds of Generosity: Are Decisions About Real and Hypothesised Money Really Different?*, Working Paper, Department of Sociology, Utrecht: University of Utrecht.

Bhati, A. and Hansen, R. (2020) "A Literature Review of Experimental Studies in Fundraising", *Journal of Behavioural Public Administration* 3 (1), 1–19.

Cagala, T., Glogowsky, U., Rincke, J. and Strittmatter, A. (2021) Optimal Targeting in Fundraising: A Machine-Learning Approach. CESifo Working Paper No. 9037, Available at SSRN http://dx.doi.org/10.2139/ssrn.3836338

Cipriano, M. and Za, S. (2021) "Exploring the Discourse on Digital Transformation in the Domain of Non-Profit Organisations. In Federica, C., Prencipe, A. and Spagnoleti, P. (Eds), *Exploring Innovation in a Digital World: Cultural and Organizational Challenges,* 198–231, Cham: Springer International Publishing.

Davies, R. and Pickering, A. (2017) *Submission to House of Lords Select Committee on Artificial Intelligence*, London: Charities Aid Foundation.

Hunt, S. (2011) "On the Intersection of Marketing History and Marketing Theory", *Marketing Theory* 11 (4), 483–489.

Jung, J., Kim, M. and Suh, J. (2022) "The Scope of 'Marketing' Research in the Nonprofit Sector: Lessons from the Last 20 Years Literature", *Journal of Philanthropy and Marketing*, e1745

Kumar, A. and Chakrabarti, S. (2023) "Charity Donor Behaviour: A Systematic Literature Review and Research Agenda", *Journal of Nonprofit and Public Sector Marketing* 35 (1), 1–46.

Lee, G., Veera Raghavan, A. and Hobbs, M. (2020) "Machine Learning the Donor Journey". In Goutte, C. and Zhu, X. (Eds), *Advances in Artificial Intelligence*, 368–374, Cham: Springer.

Lv, L. and Huang, M. (2022) "Can Personalized Recommendations in Charity Advertising Boost Donation? The Role of Perceived Autonomy", *Journal of Advertising*, Early view, 1–18.

Martinez-Levy, A., Rossi, D., Cartocci, G., Mancini, M., Di Flumeri, G., Trettel, A., Babiloni, F. and Cherubino, P. (2022) "Message Framing, Non-Conscious Perception and Effectiveness in Nonprofit Advertising. Contribution by Neuromarketing Research", *International Review on Public and Nonprofit Marketing* 19, 53–75.

Novatorov, E. (2018) "Toward Improving the Quality of Empirical Public and Nonprofit Research: Advocating for a Pluralistic Methodological Approach", *International Review on Public and Nonprofit Marketing* 15 (1), 67–86.

Shang, J., Sargeant, A. and Carpenter, K. (2019) "Giving Intention Versus Giving Behaviour: How Differently Do Satisfaction, Trust, and Commitment Relate to Them?", *Nonprofit and Voluntary Sector Quarterly* 48 (5), 1023–1044.

Taylor, R., Torugsa, N. and Arundel, A. (2017) "Leaping into Real World Relevance: An Abduction Process for Nonprofit Research", *Nonprofit and Voluntary Sector Quarterly* 47 (1), 206–227.

Vogelsang, K., Packmohr, S. and Brink, H. (2021). "Challenges of the Digital Transformation: Comparing Nonprofit and Industry Organizations". In Ahlemann, F., Schütte, R. and Stieglitz, S. (Eds), *Innovation Through Information Systems,* 297–312, Cham: Springer.

Wymer, W. (2013) "The Influence of Marketing Scholarship's Legacy on Nonprofit Marketing", *International Journal of Financial Studies* 1, 102–118.

Index

Note: Page numbers in *bold italics* refer to boxes.

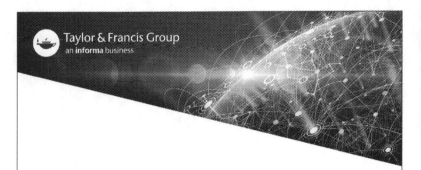

Printed in the United States
by Baker & Taylor Publisher Services